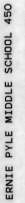

When Giant Mammals Thundered

The Cenozoic Era

Jean F. Blashfield with Richard P. Jacobs

Produced for Heinemann Library by Books Two, Inc.
Editorial: Jean Black, Deborah Grahame
Design: Michelle Lisseter
Illustrations: John T. Wallace, Top-Notch Productions
Picture Research: JLM Visuals
Production: Jean Black

Originated by Modern Age Repro
Printed and bound by South China Printing Company

10 09 08 07 06
10 9 8 7 6 5 4 3 2 1

Library of Congress Cataloging-in-Publication Data
Blashfield, Jean F.
  When giant mammals thundered : the cenozoic era/ Jean F. Blashfield and
Richard P. Jacobs.
      p. cm. -- (Prehistoric North America)
  Includes bibliographical references and index.
  ISBN 1-4034-7661-6
  1. Geology, Stratigraphic--Cenozoic--Juvenile literature. 2.
Geology--North America--Juvenile literature. 3. Plate tectonics--North
America--Juvenile literature. I. Jacobs, Richard P. II. Title. III. Series:
Blashfield, Jean F. Prehistoric North America.
  QE690.B53 2005
  560′.178--dc22

                                  2004027617

Geology consultant: Marli Bryant Miller, Ph.D., University of Oregon
Maps: Ronald C, Blakey, Ph.D., Northern Arizona University
PHOTO CREDITS: COVER: Sloth skeleton at Field Museum, Richard P. Jacobs; Mount St, Helens, Marli Miller; TITLE PAGE: Giant ground sloth, Field Museum
INTERIOR:Amundson, Burton A.: 27 bot right, 29, 32 bot; Balkwell, David: 72 Archean; Bouchery, Steve: 32 top; Crangle, Charlie: 19 bot, 54, 73 Jurassic; The Field Museum: 5, 58, 59, 60 top, 60 bot, 62 top, 62 bot, 63 top, 66 top, 65 top, 65 bot left, 66 bot, 69 top, 72 Cambrian, Silurian, Permian, 73 Paleocene, Miocene, Pliocene; Gilbert, Gordon R.: 15 top right, 19 top, 73 Eocene; Irving, Anthony: 56 top; Jacobs, Richard P.: Page borders, 10, 11 bot, 12 bot, 13 left, 15 bot left, 30 top, 39, 40, 41, 44, 45 bot, 55, 56 bot, 57, 60 mid, 61 top, 61 bot, 63 top, 64 bot left, 64 top; Kent, Breck P.: 4, 14, 15 top left, 16, 22 bot, 27 bot left, 31, 33, 50 mid, 50 bot, 56 mid, 64 bot right, 67, 72 Ordovician, Devonian, Mississippian, 73 Holocene; Larson, Alden C.: 43, 48 bot; Laudon, Lowell R.: 34, 37 top, 38 bot, 48 top; Leszczynski, Zig: 73 Oligocene; Library of Congress: 36; Miller, Marli: 45 top, 47, 73 Pleistocene; Minnich, John: 30 bot; NASA: 5 top,11 top, 13 right, 28 bot, 38 top, 42, 52; NASA/Jacques Descloitres, MODIS Land Science Team: 6; NPS: 23 bot; NEPTUNE Project and CEV: 23 top; OAR/NURP: 12 top; Smithsonian National Museum of Natural History: 72 Proterozoic, Pennsylvanian; Snead, Rodman E.: 27 top, 37 bot, 50 top; USDA: 15 bot right, 65; USF&WS: 69 bot; USGS: 24, 28 top, 46, 51; University of Michigan Exhibit Museum: 73 Triassic; Zitzer, Marypat: 7.

Some words are shown in bold, **like this**. You can find the definitions for these words in the glossary.

Contents

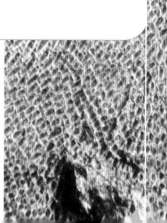

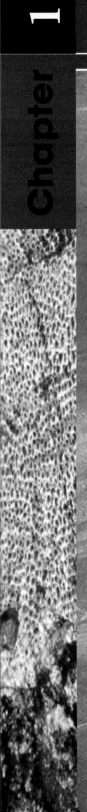

The Age of Dinosaurs ended 65 million years ago. It ended after a **meteorite** struck the Yucatan Peninsula in Mexico. The object from outer space has been called Chicxulub (pronounced CHIK-shoo-loob). The aftereffects of that strike finished off the great **reptiles**. This event is called the **Cretaceous-Tertiary** (or K-T) **Extinction**.

Various animals and plants were already becoming extinct. However, the meteorite was the final blow. It put a finish to the Mesozoic **Era** of geological history. That era had lasted 183 million years. A new era was starting, the Cenozoic Era. The Cenozoic is still going on today.

As the Cenozoic Era began, North America did not yet look as it does today. It was a smaller continent called **Laurentia** by geologists. The Atlantic Ocean had just begun to form. It already separated Africa from Laurentia, however. At the same time, South America was moving northward, closer to North America. Both Africa and South America had been part of **Gondwana**. This was the southern **supercontinent** that was still in the process of splitting up as the era began.

Impacts from Space

The Chicxulub **crater** was discovered in 1978. The discovery started a new line of research for geologists. Meteorites and other objects from space are together called **bolides**. Geologists knew that bolides occasionally hit Earth. They didn't regard these explosive visitors as very important, however.

More recently, geologists have come to see that bolides played a role in the formation of all the planets in our solar system. Even Earth's moon may have formed in a massive collision between Earth and a bolide.

↰ *Craters on the moon were formed by bolide strikes early in the solar system's history.*

↰ *Meteor Crater in Arizona is one of the few signs made recently that Earth can be struck by objects from space, or bolides. Also called Barringer Crater, it was formed 50,000 years ago.*

When a bolide strikes a planet, rock and soil are exploded away by the impact. Left behind is a bowl-shaped **basin** called a crater. In general, craters are later covered over by **sediments**. Or they may **fold** and **fault** into other shapes. Since 1950, geologists have identified at least 160 bolide impact craters.

About 35 million years ago, a bolide struck Chesapeake Bay in Virginia. The **comet** or meteorite struck with a great blaze of flame. It left a crater about 55 miles (90 km) in diameter. The evidence of that event lies beneath coastal Virginia at the mouth of Chesapeake Bay.

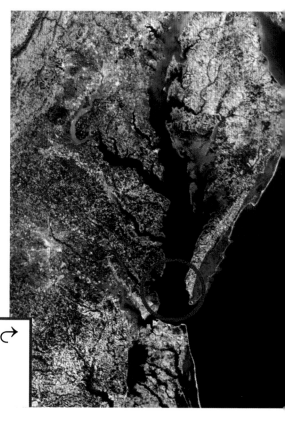

Scientists have found evidence that a bolide struck the southern end of Chesapeake Bay. The crater formed lies about 1,000 to 1,600 feet (300-500 m) below ground, approximately in the circled area.

Witnessing a Bolide Impact

A major bolide impact took place on June 30, 1908. It is the only major bolide impact for which we have eyewitness testimony. It is called the Tunguska Event. A meteor exploded in the atmosphere, about 20,000 feet (6 km) up, above Siberia, the cold northeastern region of Russia. As much as 50 miles (80 km) away, people were thrown to the ground by the force of explosive air pressure.

Witnesses more than 100 miles (161 km) away saw the fireball in the air before it exploded. No crater was formed. This is because the bolide blew up before reaching the planet's surface. It is estimated that 80 million trees were burned or blown over by the forces released by the explosion.

Geologic Time

Geologists have worked to separate different sections of Earth's history into a usable calendar called the **geologic time scale**. The large section that we are still in is called the Cenozoic **Era**, meaning "recent life" era. It is divided by most geologists into two **periods**. The Tertiary (meaning "third") is from 65 to 1.8 million years ago. The Quaternary (meaning "fourth") is from 1.8 million years ago to the present. The largest part of the Quaternary—the Pleistocene **Epoch**—is often called the **Ice Age**.

Geologists use the terms *Tertiary* and *Quaternary*, but they do not use terms that would mean "first" and "second." An 18th-century Italian miner divided geologic time into Primary, Secondary, and Tertiary. Gradually, the first two units were replaced with other terms.

We know much more about geology and the development of living things during the Cenozoic than we do about earlier eras. Therefore, the Cenozoic's periods are further divided into epochs. The name of each epoch ends in *-cene*, which means "recent."

The names of the Tertiary epochs do not tell much. The first epoch is the Paleocene, or the "old recent." The second is the Eocene, meaning "dawn." This refers to the dawning of the time in which modern mammals expanded greatly. The third epoch is the Oligocene, meaning "few." This is because there were few new mammals. The fourth is the Miocene, which means "less." It is followed by the Pliocene, which means "continuing."

The Tertiary and Quaternary are quite different in length. For this reason, some geologists replace the Tertiary Period with two periods. They put the Paleogene (meaning "old birth") as running from 65 to 23.8 million years ago. They refer to it as the "Age of Mammals." It was the major time period during which mammals evolved into the ones we know today. The Paleogene includes three of the familiar epochs: Paleocene, Eocene, and Oligocene.

↱ *The names of epochs in the Cenozoic Era refer to the evolution of mammals, such as these caribou.*

PRECAMBRIAN TIME • *4.5 billion to 543 million years ago*
PALEOZOIC ERA • *543 to 248 million years ago*
MESOZOIC ERA • *248 to 65 million years ago*

CENOZOIC ERA • *65 million years ago to present*

Time Period	Tectonic Events	Biological Events
Paleocene Epoch *65 to 54.8 million years ago*	Laramide orogeny Western Laurentia uplifted	Mammals and birds diversified First horse ancestors
Eocene Epoch *54.8 to 33.7 million years ago*	Rockies uplifted Global cooling began	First mammals (whales) in sea First primates First cats and dogs
Oligocene Epoch *33.7 to 23.8 million years ago*	North Atlantic opened Ice cap formed in Anatarctica	First apes Grasslands widespread
Miocene Epoch *23.8 to 5.3 million years ago*	Columbia flood basalts	First human ancestors First mastodons
Pliocene Epoch *5.3 to 1.8 million years ago*	Northern Hemisphere glaciation began Cascade Volcanoes	Large mammals abundant
Pleistocene Epoch *1.8 million years ago to today*	Great glaciation of Northern Hemisphere	First modern humans Extinction of large mammals Humans entered North America
Holocene *10,000 years ago to today*	Rifting continued in East Africa Human–caused global warming	Human-caused extinctions

Left margin vertical labels:
PHANEROZOIC TIME • 543 million years ago to present
CENOZOIC ERA • 65 million years ago to present
TERTIARY PERIOD • 65 to 1.8 million years ago
QUATERNARY PERIOD 1.8 million to today

The second Tertiary time period took place from 23 to 1.8 million years ago. It is called the Neogene, meaning "new birth." The Neogene includes the Miocene and the Pliocene. However, most geologists continue to use the epoch names shown above.

Swampy Land and the West

The western shores of North America were located several hundred miles east of where they are now. The Sundance Sea, also called the Western Interior Seaway, still occupied most of western North America. It left only a narrow border of land on the west side. The shallow sea had formed during the late Jurassic Period. Dinosaurs occupied the swampy lands that bordered the sea.

The Sundance Sea continued to provide a shallow **marine** environment for the first part of the Tertiary. The land that would later become the Rocky Mountains began to rise, or **uplift**. The rising land eroded. It poured vast amounts of sediment into the Sundance Sea. This uplift also made the shallow sea pour out of the continental basin it had occupied, back into the ocean.

Sediments filled in the swamps. They gradually turned to **coal** beds. Western coal mining is centered from Wyoming north. Much of the land flooded by the Sundance Sea is now North America's Great Plains.

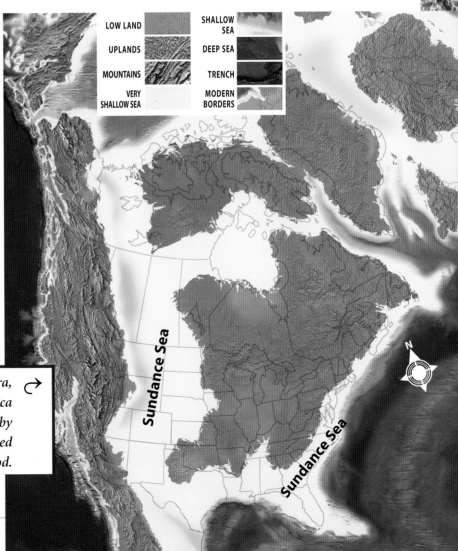

LOW LAND
UPLANDS
MOUNTAINS
VERY SHALLOW SEA
SHALLOW SEA
DEEP SEA
TRENCH
MODERN BORDERS

During the end of the Mesozoic Era, the central part of North America and the east coast were covered by the Sundance Sea. It still existed during the Tertiary Period.

↰ North America's Great Plains were once the Sundance Sea, a shallow sea that covered the central part of the continent.

There was still no California, no British Columbia, no Alaska, and no Rocky Mountains. New land was on its way, however. The Farallon plate was carrying it. This is one of the **tectonic plates** into which the planet's outer surface, or **lithosphere**, is broken.

The Farallon plate lay to the west of the North American plate. The huge Farallon plate split in two, from east to west. The southern portion was still called the Farallon. The northern portion was given the name *Kula*. During the Cenozoic, these two plates would continue to build the west coast of the continent. This process will be explained in the next chapter.

When a plate bearing ocean meets a plate bearing a continent, the more dense oceanic plate moves under the other. It moves downward into the **mantle**, in a trench or **subduction** zone. The Kula plate stopped subducting, or being pulled under, about 55 million years ago. It began to move northward. From there it was subducted under western Canada and Alaska. In addition, a new subduction zone formed in the north. Along that zone the Aleutian Islands formed. By 40 million years ago, the Kula plate had disappeared.

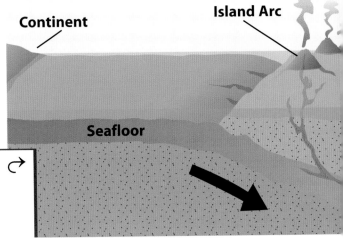

Continent

Island Arc

Seafloor

↱ A subduction zone is a trench where seafloor is drawn back into Earth's mantle. Volcanic land, called island arcs, forms as a result. Alaska's Aleutian Islands formed as such an island arc.

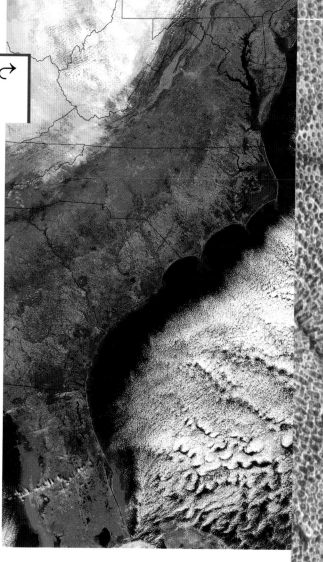

A plain built up on the eastern coast of North America. It was the Coastal Plain, shown here from space. Its southern end became Florida.

The East Coast

On the ocean side of the eastern Appalachian Mountains, sediments from erosion had been building up. This had been happening since the middle of the Cretaceous Period. These sediments continued to build during most of the Tertiary. They were building a flat, sedimentary area that would come to be called the **Coastal Plain**.

Florida was attached to the southeastern corner of the Coastal Plain. Its rock is a huge platform. Much of it is underwater. The platform consists of **limestone**. Coral and other **reef**-forming creatures formed the limestone. The Florida platform was originally attached to Africa as part of Gondwana. When Laurentia pulled away from Gondwana and moved northward, it pulled the Florida platform along with it.

For millions of years, limestone continued to accumulate on the Florida platform. This happened especially through the Eocene. Later, clay and other sediments covered the limestone. These had eroded from the newly uplifted Appalachians. Florida as we know it today lies on the eastern side of the platform.

The eastern Coastal Plain is the flat area along the coast where sediments eroded from the Appalachian Mountains collected. This is North Carolina's Coastal Plain.

Seeing the Bedrock of Southern Florida

Much of Florida is barely above sea level. The elevation is a little higher in the northern part of the state. South of Lake Okeechobee the elevation seldom exceeds 25 feet (7.6 m) above sea level. The elevation of the Florida Keys averages less than half that.

The **bedrock** of this low, flat land is almost entirely limestone. This indicates that the Florida peninsula had once been submerged in a shallow sea environment. Some of the limestone consists primarily of the **calcite** external skeletons of such animals as coral, or the shells of other marine animals. Others are composed of tiny, round grains of nonbiological calcite cemented together.

The skeletons of coral, sponges, and other marine animals form most of Florida's limestone. ↻

Limestone forms the base of the Florida peninsula. ↓

12

Limestone outcrops, or exposed portions of layers, are seen in many of the drainage canals along the roads of southern Florida. Others are exposed in the marshes and swamps of the Everglades. Quarrying, or cutting away the stone, exposes the reef limestone of the Florida Keys at Windley Key Fossil Reef Geological State Park.

Sometimes surface limestone suddenly collapses. This creates a sinkhole into which cars and even houses can fall.

Chunks of limestone are exposed in the Everglades. ↘

Many of Florida's lakes were formed as sinkholes, where the limestone collapsed. ↑

Freeing the Mammals

Until the Cretaceous-Tertiary Extinction dinosaurs ruled the land. **Mammals** existed, but they were small and elusive, or hard to find. One of the earliest true mammals was a small creature similar to a shrew. Called *Megazostrodon*, it appeared during the Triassic Period of the Mesozoic. Dinosaurs dominated the scene, so mammals did not grow much bigger. Mammals survived the K-T Extinction and began to change and grow.

Mammals already occupied all the continents when the dinosaurs disappeared. The mammals were suddenly free to take over habitats previously occupied by the land-living reptiles. Mammals evolved fairly quickly into many different kinds and sizes. The main advantage the mammals had over the dinosaurs was **adaptability**. They were able to adjust to sudden major changes in climate or habitat.

The mammals that existed when the Cenozoic started had some important differences among them. Some of them were **marsupials**. These are mammals that give birth to very immature young. The young then develop inside the mother's pouch. (*Marsupium* means "pouch.") Others were **placental mammals**. The young of these mammals develop within the female and are nourished by a temporary special organ called a placenta.

Marsupials could not succeed against placental mammals. The young of placental mammals are much more highly developed at birth. They are more likely than marsupials to grow up and reproduce.

A few marsupials are still found in the Americas. The opossum of North America is an example. The marsupials' lasting success occurred only in Australia. They reached that continent through Antarctica. This happened when Australia was still connected to the polar continent. Separation began toward the end of the Mesozoic and ended about 55 million years ago.

The opossum, North America's only marsupial, occupies most states except in desert regions.

Monotremes are mammals that don't fit either the marsupial or the placental category. The only two monotremes are the platypus (left) and the spiny anteater, or echidna (above). They lay eggs and produce milk. Babies lap it from the mother's skin.

The mammals that developed after the K-T Extinction lived primarily in forests. These forests had spread throughout much of the world at the end of the Cretaceous. Their trees belonged to a new kind of plant called **angiosperms**. Angiosperms are flowering plants. They have seeds enclosed in a case. Their flowers provided an opportunity for greater genetic variety than the older ferns and **conifers**.

The Cenozoic Era was set to bring as many changes to Earth and its continents as earlier eras had.

Sunflowers are angiosperms that develop their seeds in a cluster in the middle of the blossom.

This fossilized maple seed is like the ones we find today.

Chapter 2

Plates on the Move: Faults and Mountains

When the Cenozoic Era began, the supercontinent **Pangea** was not through breaking up into the continents we know now. The huge tectonic plates that make up the lithosphere of the planet were on the move.

The Atlantic Ocean had begun to open up in the central region, near the Gulf of Mexico. But North America and Europe remained attached to each other at Scandinavia. Greenland lay in between. North American and Europe had been attached throughout at least 350 million years of Earth's history. They moved in and out of various supercontinents.

During the late Mesozoic Era, **rifts** began to form in several places in the seafloor around Labrador and Greenland. Rifts are areas of **crust** that lie above a **heat plume** in the mantle. The heat causes the crust to stretch and break. **Lava** can ooze out of the break. If such stretching goes on for a long enough time, the lava can form oceanic crust. A new ocean is formed. However, the Mesozoic rifts failed to continue.

Separating Europe and North America

About 60 million years ago, a new rift formed between Greenland and Scandinavia. This time the rift continued long enough. The northern part of the Atlantic Ocean was born.

Lava poured through the fissure, or narrow opening, in the rift. This became a **seafloor spreading** ridge between Europe and North America. Called the Mid-Atlantic Ridge, it became permanent about 35 million years ago. The spreading ridge in the northern Atlantic joined up with one in the central Atlantic, which had formed during the Mesozoic Era.

The Mid-Atlantic Ridge still creates new seafloor. Greenland and Scandinavia are still moving apart. This separation occurs at a rate of less than an inch (2 cm) per year.

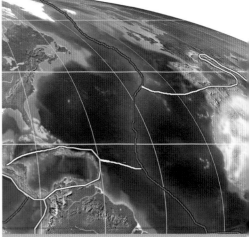

↰ *The red line on this globe section is the seafloor spreading ridge called the Mid-Atlantic Ridge.*

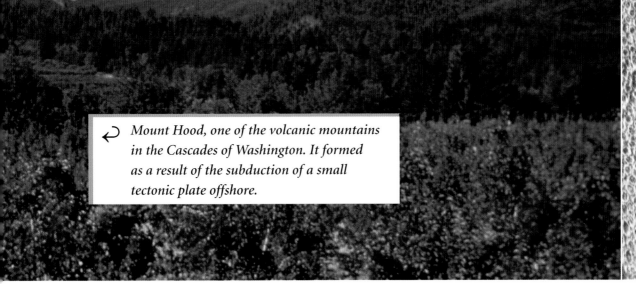

↰ *Mount Hood, one of the volcanic mountains in the Cascades of Washington. It formed as a result of the subduction of a small tectonic plate offshore.*

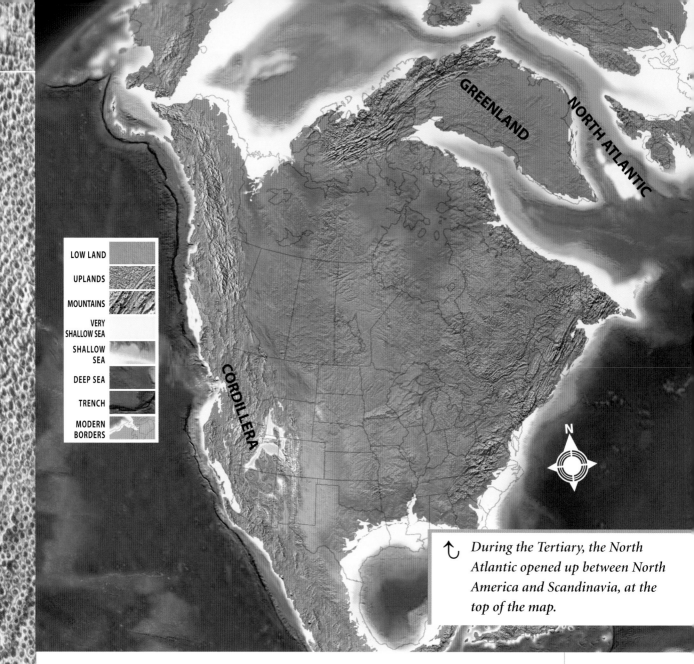

LOW LAND
UPLANDS
MOUNTAINS
VERY SHALLOW SEA
SHALLOW SEA
DEEP SEA
TRENCH
MODERN BORDERS

GREENLAND

NORTH ATLANTIC

CORDILLERA

N

During the Tertiary, the North Atlantic opened up between North America and Scandinavia, at the top of the map.

Another result of this new rifting is the fascinating island of Iceland. This land was formed only about 20 million years ago. It is actually part of the Mid-Atlantic Ridge itself. An active volcanic zone runs through the middle of the island. It continues to ooze lava.

The heat in the mantle beneath Iceland is quite close to the surface. As a result, the underground water in much of Iceland is heated by nature. The Icelanders use this natural hot water to heat their homes. Despite all the heat, Iceland has many **glaciers**. These gave the island its name.

The rift in the Mid-Atlantic Ridge, from which lava can pour, is visible in the island of Iceland.

Iceland is located half on the North American plate and half on the Eurasian plate. In the middle of the island people can actually walk between the two different plates. This is one of the few places on Earth where that is possible.

Mountains in Eurasia

The plates opening up the northern Atlantic continued to move—and still move today. But this was not the only place where plates were moving. The biggest **orogeny**, or mountain-building episode, of the Cenozoic Era is still taking place in the Himalayan mountain belt north of India.

Pieces of Gondwana, the old southern supercontinent, drifted northward. This was happening about 55 million years ago. Finally, during the Eocene Epoch, the large landmass now called India struck the Eurasian plate. The collision thrust the Himalayan mountain chain upward. This event made them the tallest mountains on Earth. The land is still rising.

The Himalayas are the newest, tallest, and most rugged mountains on Earth. They have had no time to erode.

The African landmass had long been part of Gondwana. It moved away from Europe and then moved back north again. Its collision with Europe raised the Alps Mountains out of crust that had been part of the seafloor. The boot-shaped landmass that is Italy had been part of Africa. It remained attached to Europe when Africa moved away again. During the last 20 million years, the remnant of the ancient Tethys Ocean between Europe and Africa has gradually turned into today's Mediterranean Sea.

The Disappearing Farallon

Mountains were also being built on the western side of Laurentia, or North America. The Pacific Coast of North America stretches from Mexico to the top of Alaska. It became part of the continent only in the last 65 million years. This region is called the **Cordillera**.

↺ *Reefs, made by coral and other animals, form around a volcanic island. As the volcano ages and sinks, masses of coral limestone remain. Such islands and reefs became exotic terrane.* ↻

The rock of the Cordillera originated thousands of miles away. Some of it consisted of island-arc volcanoes. These formed in the sea when an oceanic plate was subducting. Other rock was formed from limestone reefs. These were built around such volcanoes. Gradually this assortment of material was gathered into rocky islands. The islands were moved by a tectonic plate toward North America. They moved as if they were being carried on a conveyor belt.

Most of the islands gradually **accreted**, or attached, to the continent. This new land is described as **exotic terrane**. It eventually became the western states and provinces of the United States, Canada, and Mexico.

The islands were carried on an ancient plate geologists call the Farallon. The North American plate, bearing Laurentia, had been moving westward for millions of years. At the same time, the Farallon plate moved eastward. As the Cenozoic began, the Farallon was being subducted beneath the North American plate. The Pacific plate was moving along behind it. There was a seafloor spreading center between them.

↶ *As the North American plate moved westward, the Farallon plate was subducted. The Pacific plate's seafloor spreading zone (the red bars) formed California's San Andreas Fault.*

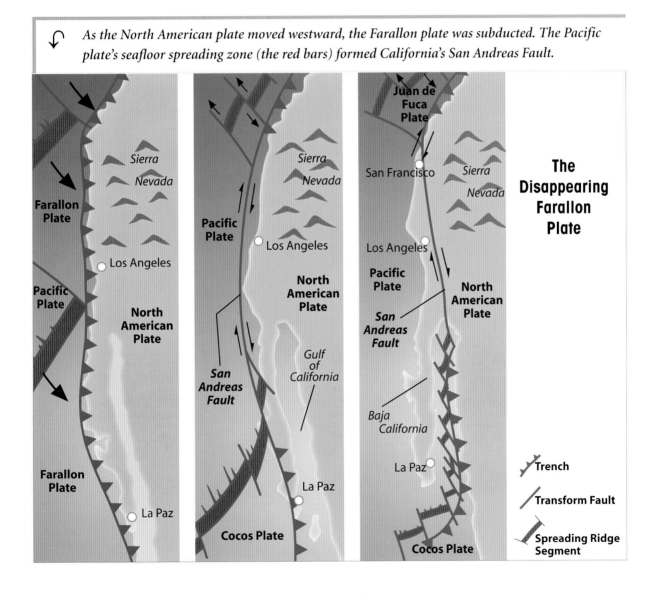

The Disappearing Farallon Plate

By 35 million years ago, during the Oligocene Epoch, the Farallon had already been subducting for a long time. As a result, the leading edge of the North American plate moved over the spreading center between the Farallon and the Pacific plates. The Farallon plate itself had mostly disappeared. It left some small remnants to the north and south. This occurred about 18 million years ago.

An important remnant of the Farallon plate is the Juan de Fuca plate. (Juan de Fuca was a Greek explorer sailing for Mexico in the 1590s.) This small plate is located by the Pacific Northwest in the United States and the southern part of British Columbia in Canada. The subduction of the Juan de Fuca plate is still causing volcanic action in the region. It is building the Cascade Range. The 500-mile (805-km)-long Cascades lie about 150 miles (241 km) inland from the ocean. They stretch from northern California into southern British Columbia.

Mount St. Helens in Washington's Cascades erupted explosively in 1980. Lassen Peak in northern California erupted throughout much of 1914 and 1915. The United States Geological Survey (USGS) maintains a web site about the individual volcanoes of the Cascade Range.

↶ *Since the big eruption of Mount St. Helens in 1980, a lava dome has been building in the volcano's crater. It still steams and smokes.*

Studying the Juan de Fuca Plate

Project NEPTUNE stands for North-East Pacific Time-series Undersea Networked Experiments. The project calls for 30 robotic deep-sea observatories. These will be placed about 62 miles (100 km) apart. They will spread across the underwater surface of the Juan de Fuca plate. The observatories will record earthquakes, volcanic eruptions, and other actions of the oceanic crust. This huge research project is being organized by both U.S. and Canadian laboratories. Scientists hope to have the network ready to operate in 2007. Researchers and classrooms around the world will be able to tune into what the instruments are recording.

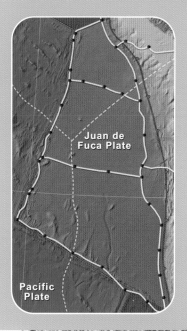

Juan de Fuca Plate

Pacific Plate

Part of the Cascades is not volcanic in origin, though it includes some volcanoes. This part, called the North Cascades, is **metamorphic rock**. The crust was thrust up into the sky when an exotic terrane struck the continent. The peaks in the North Cascades are steeper than the other mountains in the area. These mountains lie just south of the Canadian border in Washington. The vast wilderness of glaciers and waterfalls is incorporated into North Cascades National Park. Two major volcanoes—Mount Baker and Glacier Peak—are in the North Cascades.

Most of the rugged peaks in North Cascades National Park are steep-sided and spectacular. ↱

The Juan de Fuca plate is created at a spreading ridge. About 300 miles (500 km) long, it lies next to the Pacific plate. It also moves away from the ridge. It subducts beneath the North American plate from north of Vancouver Island to Mendocino, California. This subduction often causes earthquakes and volcanoes in Washington and British Columbia.

Another remnant of the Farallon plate is the Cocos plate. It is located off Mexico and Central America. It is subducting beneath the Caribbean plate. Here it, too, causes volcanoes and earthquakes.

Transform Fault

The break in the Earth's crust called the San Andreas Fault cuts through much of California. It is a long transform fault along which the North American plate and the Pacific plate slide past each other during earthquakes.

The San Andreas Fault

As described earlier, the North American plate moved over the spreading center between the Farallon and the Pacific plates. The spreading center itself was mostly subducted. The part that was not subducted changed from a seafloor spreading zone to a transform fault. This happened between 15 and 20 million years ago.

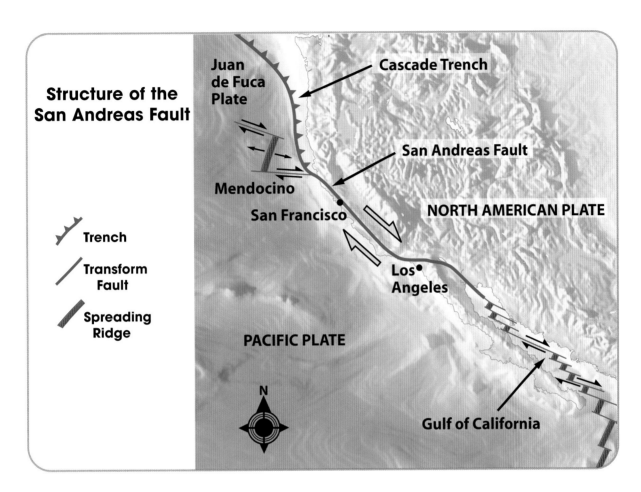

Structure of the San Andreas Fault

Juan de Fuca Plate

Cascade Trench

San Andreas Fault

Mendocino

San Francisco

NORTH AMERICAN PLATE

Trench

Transform Fault

Spreading Ridge

Los Angeles

PACIFIC PLATE

N

Gulf of California

A fault covering a long distance breaks into a series of shorter faults that go crosswise. This is because of the curvature of Earth's surface. These breaks are called transform faults. They make the longer fault appear as a series of zigzags across the curvature of the planet. The Pacific and North American plates meet along a boundary that is now a series of transform faults instead of a trench.

The longest fault of the boundary between the two plates is the San Andreas Fault. It begins at the subduction zone of the Juan de Fuca plate at Mendocino, California. The fault continues southward to a series of short spreading ridges in the Gulf of California. This structure means that a long narrow strip of the western side of California lies on the Pacific plate. The rest of California lies on the North American plate.

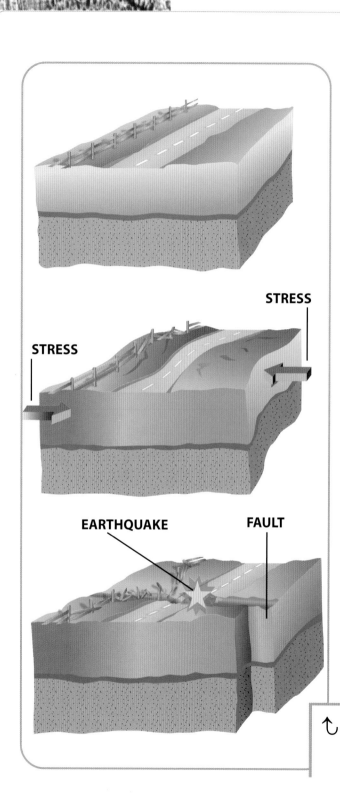

STRESS

STRESS

EARTHQUAKE

FAULT

The Gulf of California began to open up about 30 million years ago. The movement of the San Andreas Fault pulled away a chunk of Mexico. (This is Baja—meaning *lower*—California, the southern peninsula that belongs to Mexico.) Movement along the fault has carried the chunk more than 300 miles (500 km) from where it started.

Unfortunately, there's often nothing smooth and quiet about the movement of rock at the San Andreas Fault. The rock along the fault "wants" to move. It is often locked in position, however. Suddenly the stress becomes too much. The rock on the Pacific plate side lurches. This is an earthquake.

When an earthquake occurs along the San Andreas fault, the fault acts as a **strike-slip fault**. In such a fault, one side moves horizontally in comparison to the other. Over the centuries, the outer portion of California has been moving northward in comparison to the main body of North America.

When stresses become too great within the crust, rock may break to relieve the stress. This sudden breaking is an earthquake.

Seeing Features of the San Andreas Fault

The San Andreas Fault of California is about 600 miles (966 km) long. From ground level, its location is not always obvious. Roadcuts running through the fault, however, expose folded, fractured, and pulverized rock.

From the air, the fault is well-marked by a north-south line of narrow ridges, valleys, and lakes. The channels of streams crossing the fault can be seen to have been moved sharply to the north. This indicates the motion along the fault. The land on the west side of the fault is moving northward relative to that on the east side. The northern end of the fault disappears into the ocean at Mendocino. Rocks at Mendocino match those over 300 miles (483 km) south. This matching shows that the rocks were once in the same location.

↻ Gnarled rock shown by a roadcut along the fault

↩ From the air

San Andreas Lake fills the fault zone south of San Francisco ↻

When the Earth Trembled in 1906

The great San Francisco Earthquake took place in 1906. The quake moved the land on the western side of the San Andreas Fault by a giant leap of 21 feet (6.4 m). That is the largest amount ever measured for land movement caused by an earthquake. People assumed that this single earthquake was the only one needed to relieve the stresses in the crust forever. Then geologists began to realize that the San Andreas Fault is just one fault in a major system of faults underlying California. Geologists and Californians expect another big earthquake to happen "soon." It will be at least as powerful as the 1906 quake.

Vancouver Island lies north of Washington State. It is located off the coast of British Columbia. The island consists of the top of volcanic mountains. These were formed beginning about 360 million years ago. It was added to by limestone and then more volcanic action. Eventually, it was moved on the Farallon plate to the west coast of North America. It became part of the huge Wrangellia exotic terrane. This terrane formed much of Alaska and western Canada. It is still moving.

Canada's major earthquake fault zone is called the Queen Charlotte Fault. It lies along the edge of Vancouver Island. Canada's largest recorded earthquake took place in 1949 along the Queen Charlotte Fault. It was felt south into Oregon.

Queen Charlotte Fault, Canada's largest, lies along Vancouver Island.

VANCOUVER ISLAND

Western Mountains

Earthquakes were not the only effect the subduction of the Farallon plate had on the west coast. North of the San Andreas Fault, the subduction of the plates uplifted mountains along the coasts. These mountains are part of the Pacific Coast Ranges. Compared to the Cascades, which are farther inland, the Coast Ranges are quite low. They average about 3,300 feet (1,000 m).

The mountains of the Coast Ranges are separated from the Sierra Nevada by a low, flat valley. (*Sierra* means "mountains" in Spanish, so it isn't necessary to say "Sierra Nevada Mountains.") In California, this valley is called the Central Valley. It covers about 18,000 square miles (47,000 sq km). The Central Valley is the primary agricultural region of California. Until about 6 million years ago, it was an ocean bay.

↺ *The flat and fertile Central Valley of California was an ocean bay before the Sierra Nevada rose.*

The Sierra Nevada make up the longest chain of mountains located only within the United States. The chain is 400 miles (644 km) long. It runs north to south along the eastern border of California. The **granite** rock of the Sierra Nevada was formed during the Mesozoic Era. It began to uplift about 6 million years ago.

The Sierra Nevada are among the most dramatic examples of **fault-block mountains** in North America. Sometimes stress on crust will make it fracture, or fault, instead of fold. When that happens, huge blocks of rock rise upward as mountains.

The Lowest Spot in North America

Death Valley is the hottest, driest, and lowest location in the Western Hemisphere. Formed by rifting, it lies 282 feet (86 m) below sea level. Its formation started when fault-block mountains rose on each side of it. Fault blocks require that the adjacent, or neighboring, crust fall. That's exactly what Death Valley did. The mountains on the west side rose and then eroded. Vast amounts of sediment have been carried into the valley. The bedrock of Death Valley lies beneath about 9,000 feet (2,740 m) of sediment.

The entire Sierra Nevada region was uplifted at an angle. The region now rises abruptly on the east side. It then tilts down to the west at a shallower angle. The entire Sierra Nevada area has risen 1.3 miles (2,092 m). This occurred over the last 10 million years. Glaciers carved deep beautiful canyons out of preexisting river valleys.

Three national parks lie within the rugged and beautiful Sierra Nevada—Yosemite, Kings Canyon, and Sequoia. Mount Whitney is located at the southern end of the Sierra Nevada chain on the eastern edge of Sequoia National Park. It is the highest peak in the main 48 states. Mount Whitney rises to 14,495 feet (4,418 m).

A glacial lake formed near Mount Whitney in the Sierra Nevada ↪

The Sierra Nevada

The uplift of the Sierra Nevada began about 25 million years ago. At that time, a large block of crust tilted westward. This occurred when it broke free along a system of faults on its eastern side. The fault system is still active today. The mountains have steep slopes on the faulted eastern side. The slopes on the western side are more gentle. **Sedimentary rock** layers overlay the tilted western side.

   Most rock in the range is either granite or described as being granitelike. This means that it is an **igneous rock** containing a great deal of **silica**. The rock was formed from a large mass of **magma**. This magma must have cooled slowly several miles beneath the surface of the planet. Erosion then removed the overlying rock before the mass of granite was exposed. Such rock is called a **batholith**.

   Domes of granite are common in the Sierra Nevada. The rounded domes were formed when erosion removed weight from the underlying rock. That rock could then expand outward and fracture into large rounded shapes.

↩   The granite batholith of the Sierra Nevada

↻ *The famous rock called Half Dome at Yosemite National Park*

Mountains are uplifted when magma within the crust makes the surface rock swell and rise. Sometimes that magma does not erupt onto the surface. Instead, it hardens into an **intrusive** igneous rock within the crust. (Rock is intrusive when it pushes into rock that already exists.) Such a body of rock is called a batholith. The beautiful Sierra Nevada is made up of a huge batholith. The surface rock has eroded, exposing the granite batholith. The famous domes of Yosemite National Park are parts of the batholith. Half Dome is a dome that split in half vertically. It is one of the park's most famous landmarks.

The Gold Rush

Veins in the batholith of the Sierra Nevada filled with quartz, a silica mineral. This quartz bore gold along with it. Erosion often released chunks of pure gold. Rivers carried these chunks. The discovery of such free gold started the California Gold Rush in 1848, bringing people to pan for gold (right). Ultimately, one-third of all United States gold came from the Sierra Nevada. It's been said that the gold provided the funds for the North to fight the South in the Civil War.

The Devils Postpile

During the late Cenozoic Era, outpourings of lava associated with the Sierra Nevada uplift occurred. A portion of a lava flow in southern California covered what is now known as Devils Postpile National Monument.

Basalt lava contracted as it cooled and hardened. The contraction caused large vertical cracks in the basalt. The cracking created six-sided columns of rock. They extend from top to bottom of the lava flow. This is a depth of more than 50 feet (15 m). Individual columns weathered and broke loose from the flow. These can be seen lying at its base.

Looking at the top surface of the flow, the columns are seen to be about 2 or 3 feet (60 to 90 cm) across. The top surface was polished and scratched by glaciers. These glaciers moved across the postpile basalt during the Ice Age.

Chapter 3

Plates on the Move: Uplifting the Rockies

Most mountain ranges in the Cordilleran region were pushed up when large **terranes** carried on the Farallon plate crashed into the North American continental plate in a huge collision. As we have seen, the new terranes added new territory to the continent. This occurred as they pushed old rock up into mountains.

The Rocky Mountains of North America are different, however. The area where they were built was a long way inland from the plate margin.

During the Mesozoic Era, vast quantities of sediments were eroded from the new volcanic and collision mountains of the Cordillera. The eroded material was carried eastward by rivers and wind. It piled up as much as 2 miles (3 km) thick and hardened into rock.

Something unusual happened to the subducting Farallon plate. The angle at which the plate went under the continent changed. It became shallower until it descended into the mantle at probably less than a 10-degree angle.

Why this happened is not certain. It might have been caused by an increase in the velocity of the subducting plate. Whatever the reason was, it meant that the region of volcanoes and earthquakes, which accompanies subduction, occurred farther inland than usual.

This mountain-building event is called the Laramide orogeny. It constructed the Rocky Mountains. From the Arctic Ocean to the Gulf of Mexico, the Rocky Mountains form the backbone of North America.

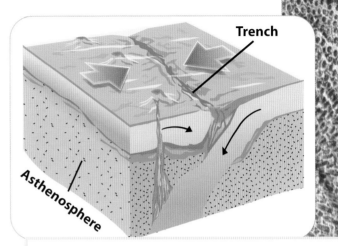

Trench

Asthenosphere

↻ *A tectonic plate is subducted when it is drawn underneath another plate and back into the mantle. A change in the angle at which a plate was subducted may have helped build the Rocky Mountains.*

↩ *The Rocky Mountains extend from Alaska southward to Mexico. This mountain lake is in the Yukon Territory of Canada.*

Letting the Wagon Trains Through

There is a low spot, or break, in the long Rocky Mountain chain. This break is called South Pass. It has an elevation of 7,500 feet (2,300 m). Its existence allowed wagon trains traveling the Oregon Trail in the 1850s to pass between the much higher mountains that surrounded them. Fort Laramie, Wyoming, was located at the eastern end of South Pass. Its name was given to the great orogeny that created the Rockies, the Laramide orogeny. Shown is an early photo of rocks in Laramie Valley.

An uplifted area called the Ancestral Rockies had been raised during the Paleozoic Era. Even before that uplift ended, the raised area was being scoured flat by wind and water. Then, in the late Cretaceous, the deep layers of sediment began to be thrust eastward by forces from the west.

The eastern region of the Rocky Mountains is called the **fold-thrust** belt. Forces from underground folded sedimentary rock. But then they also pushed it eastward over other rock. Frequently, the rock in the thrust belt eroded into rugged, jagged edges of the sedimentary rock. Recent erosion made the eastern side of the Rockies particularly spectacular. This east side is called the Front Range. Glacier National Park in Montana also has some amazingly jagged mountains. These were formed by thrust and erosion.

The eastern Rockies were created by forces that both folded the rock and thrust it over other rock.

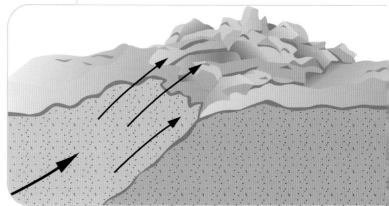

About 30 million years ago, the land calmed. But the Rockies were not yet the mountains we know. What we see today is the result of later faulting and carving. The force of moving glaciers carried out the carving processes during the last 2 million years.

The Brooks Range in northern Alaska is part of the Rockies.

The northernmost extension of the Rocky Mountains is the Brooks Range in Alaska. The rock had been a clutter of low-lying mountains in the Arctic waters. During the Jurassic, a moving tectonic plate gathered up that land. The movement started to pile rock up into mountains. This 700-mile (1,125-km)-wide range now makes up the bulk of northern Alaska. On its northern side stretches a huge coastal plain that reaches to the Arctic Sea. This becomes the North Slope, the broad plain of permanently frozen soil called **tundra**.

The remainder of Alaska is made up of a collection of exotic terranes. Collisions of those terranes occurred during later periods. These collisions built additional mountains to the south. The White Mountains and then the Alaska Range gradually filled in the state. As many as 50 exotic terranes may have collected to assemble it.

The community of Barrow, Alaska, seen here from the air, thrives on pumping oil from the North Slope.

The northern side of the Pacific plate is still subducting under the part of the North American plate that extends westward into Asia. This subduction process formed the Aleutian Islands, Alaska's western "tail."

The Canadian Rockies

The Rocky Mountains of western Canada consist of long and narrow mountain ranges. These extend in an approximate northwest-southeast direction. They are bordered on the east by the interior plains. A major fault in Earth's crust is called the Rocky Mountain Trench. This system of valleys lies on the west side of the Rockies. It stretches lengthwise through British Columbia, more than 1,000 miles (1,600 km). Geologists are not certain what caused the trench to form.

↵ The Rocky Mountain Trench seen from space

The rock of these mountains is sedimentary rock of marine origin. One of the most common is **shale**. Faulting and some folding of the sedimentary layers are evident. These show that the mountains were formed by horizontal compression. The compression was so great as to cause **thrust faults**. This occurred where huge areas of deeper, older rock layers were pushed up and over younger rock. The rock contains many **fossils**.

↑ Shale-covered slopes of the Canadian Rockies have revealed fossils of ancient life.

More recently, **glaciation** has greatly affected the appearance of these mountains. The ice has carved sharp mountain peaks along with U-shaped valleys. Many glaciers remain and can be easily seen. Canada has five spectacular national parks within the Rockies.

↳ The rough Rockies of Banff National Park, Canada's first national park

Starting about 30 million years ago, the entire western portion of the continent began to rise. This uplift included the region from the Mackenzie Delta in northwestern Canada to Mexico and from Nevada east to the Mississippi River. There were few major changes in the landscape. It was a general uplift of the entire scene.

This uplift raised the Rockies even higher than they had been. It created North America's Continental Divide. This is the high-elevation line that determines which way rivers flow. Rain that falls to the east of the Continental Divide eventually ends up in the Atlantic Ocean. Rain that falls to the west ends up in the Pacific.

The Colorado Plateau

A **plateau** is an area of generally flat rock that has been uplifted above the surrounding land. It often has steep sides like cliffs. The largest one in North America is the Colorado Plateau. Actually, it is made up of many different plateaus. Together, these plateaus cover about 140,000 square miles (362,600 sq km). Altogether, they occupy much of Colorado, New Mexico, Arizona, and Utah.

↑ *This spectacular part of the Colorado Plateau in Utah is made up of many smaller plateaus.*

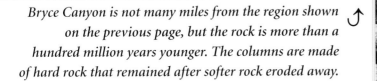

Bryce Canyon is not many miles from the region shown on the previous page, but the rock is more than a hundred million years younger. The columns are made of hard rock that remained after softer rock eroded away.

The metamophic rock of the plateau is ancient. Its base was formed more than 1.7 billion years ago. After that, layer after layer of sediments settled on top of it. This occurred as the plateau resided below various seas. When the Cenozoic Era began, sediment had reached nearly to sea level.

During the Tertiary, the whole region was uplifted. The plateau reached an elevation ranging between 3,940 to 5,900 feet (1,200-1,800 m) above sea level. Many volcanoes formed along regions of major faulting.

The Colorado Plateau remained intact and stable while the Rocky Mountains were being built to the east of it. This was also the case as the Basin and Range region (see the next page) was being stretched and moved to the west of it. Eventually, the entire western part of North America was uplifted even farther. This happened about 10 million years ago.

Overall, the Colorado Plateau remained unchanged during this activity. Its shape is generally flat, but it is made up of many different smaller plateaus. There are also many folds and faults. The plateau includes deep canyons, volcanic mountains, and beautiful red rocks. The Colorado River cut down through the many layers of sedimentary rock. This created the world-famous Grand Canyon.

There are fifteen different national parks and national monuments in the area. These protect and allow visitors to easily view the spectacular landscape of the Colorado Plateau.

The Basin and Range Province

The whole of Nevada, southern Arizona, plus parts of adjacent states, make up a geologic section of North America called the Basin and Range **Province**. It consists of lines of mountain ranges, running north to south. Between the ranges lie valleys.

Heat plumes in the mantle made the crust stretch. **Normal faults** formed, and some rock rose into mountains. Meanwhile, other rock dropped, forming valleys. Over the following millions of years, sediment that eroded from the mountains collected in the valleys, or basins. The rifting that formed the province failed to break apart the continent. But it left more than a hundred of these narrow mountain ranges, with wide, flat basins separating them.

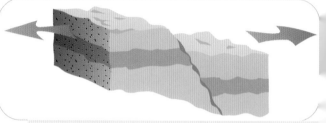

↶ *As the crust stretched, it broke into a series of normal faults.*

The Basin and Range Province started to form during the Miocene Epoch and is still forming, as well as growing. Geologists say that the rock it was made from stretched 100 percent from east to west. This doubled the area's size and changed the shape of the North American continent.

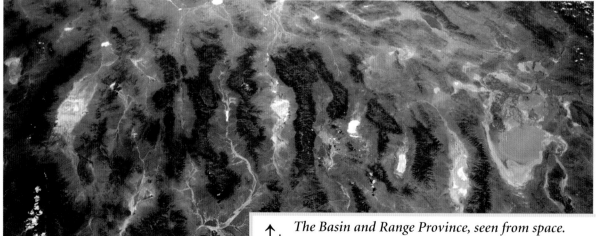

↶ *The Basin and Range Province, seen from space. The dark north-south "stripes" are the mountain ranges, separated by sediment-filled basins.*

Devils Tower

Devils Tower National Monument is located in the northeast corner of Wyoming. The top of the "tower" is about 860 feet (262 m) above its base. It can be seen at a great distance as it rises high above the Great Plains. The top has an area of about 1.5 acres (0.6 ha).

Devils Tower consists of columns of igneous rock. These columns rise above the surrounding sedimentary layers. Individual columns are up to 15 feet (4.6 m) across. The steep sides of the structure make it a favorite of rock climbers.

It was long thought that Devils Tower was the plug or neck of an early Tertiary volcano. Now it is thought to have formed when magma was forced into overlying layers of sedimentary rock. That surrounding rock has since eroded.

The Great Plains of North America begins at the eastern front of the Rocky Mountains. This scene is in Alberta, Canada.

The Great Plains

The Great Plains of North America occupy the central portion of the continent. They stretch north from Mexico into Canada and eastward from the Rocky Mountains. This area is quite flat and stable. Underlying the Plains is the **craton**. This is the old original rock of the continent. It has not been disturbed by mountain-building pressures either from the east or the west. But that doesn't mean it hasn't changed.

As soon as the Rocky Mountains started rising, they began to erode. Most of the sediment developed by wind and weather was carried by rivers to the east. It built up in thick layers of sedimentary rock over the craton.

The Great Plains is certainly not without some special features. Spectacular things can happen to rock. The Devils Tower in Wyoming and the Badlands of South Dakota are examples.

It is on the Great Plains and the flat land to the east of the Plains that grasslands developed during the Cenozoic. The plains and their grasses provided a huge new environment. Many plant-eating and running animals were able to develop there.

The Badlands

The Badlands of South Dakota consist of such sedimentary rock as **mudstone** and shale. These fine-grained rock layers were formed from deposits of clay and silt, along with some volcanic ash. The Badlands' clay and silt came from erosion of the Rocky Mountains. The ash from volcanic eruptions also contributed. These events took place during the Oligocene. The fine texture of the rock indicates that the sediments were deposited on a swampy **floodplain**. A floodplain is a low, flat area near a stream. It becomes covered with water when the stream overflows its banks.

   After the mudstones and shale had formed, uplift of the area caused running water to begin eating away at the rocks. Steep and barren slopes were formed in the fine-grained rock layers. This formation created the type of scenery that we call "badlands."

↳ A scene in South Dakota's Badlands

↳ Giant pig skull from the Badlands

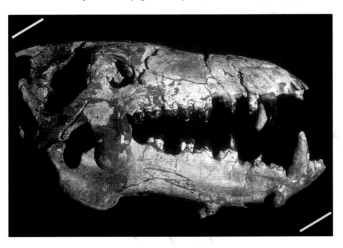

Today, Badlands National Park is an eerie combination of rough, eroded rock and prairie grasses. Important deposits of mammal fossils have been found in the Badlands. They show the evolution of various animals such as horses, pigs, and rhinoceroses. A major collection of these skeletons is found at the museum of the South Dakota School of Mines and Technology in Rapid City.

Chapter 4

Hot Spots and Volcanoes

Many of the landforms of our planet have resulted from **molten** rock, or lava, pushing its way out of the crust. Molten rock has been liquefied by heat. We tend to think of lava as forming and flowing out of cone-shaped mountains. But lava can flow out of any weak spot in the lithosphere. It may ooze out in long-lasting eruptions called **flood basalts**. Basalt is the main volcanic, or igneous, rock that makes up ocean floor. This dark gray rock can also flow out on land.

Some of the biggest flood basalts are called **traps**. That name is from the Swedish word *trapp*, meaning "staircase." This is because flood basalts tend to form in steplike layers. The Siberian Traps gave off poisonous fumes. These played a role in the great **Permian Extinction**, which ended the Paleozoic Era. The Deccan Traps of India may have played a similar role in ending the Mesozoic's Age of Dinosaurs.

North America has its flood basalt, too, though it was not as huge as those of Siberia and India. Lava flowed out of the earth, starting in the Miocene Epoch and lasting several million years. It flowed through long rifts in the crust in what is now the Pacific Northwest. The lava covered an area of about 200,000 square miles (520,000 sq km). It piled up a layer more than 10,000 feet (3,000 m) thick. Earth's crust sank beneath the weight of the basalt. The flood basalt formed the region now known as the Columbia Plateau. The vast plateau lies between the Cascade Mountains on the west and the Rocky Mountains on the east. The Columbia River runs through it.

↻ *Layers of basalt rock formed on the Columbia Plateau in Washington when lava oozed through the crust.*

↩ *Mount St. Helens, in the Cascade Mountains of Washington State, erupted in 1980 after being quiet for 123 years. Huge quantities of ash were spewed into the air and circled the globe.*

A Plateau of Lava

The area covering much of Washington and Oregon, as well as southern Idaho, was once flooded by basalt lava. Layer upon layer of basalt can be seen in the walls of the canyons. The region is called the Columbia Plateau.

The basalt was formed by outpourings of lava during the late Tertiary, especially during the Miocene. The lava did not flow from volcanoes. Instead, it flowed from large fissures, or cracks, now buried under the flows. Some of the lava must have traveled a great distance before it cooled and solidified.

One flow started in Idaho and traveled the 370 miles (600 km) to the Pacific. This is the longest known lava flow on Earth.

There were many successive flows. In some places, more than 20 separate flows are piled one on top of the other, forming steps. Later folding and faulting affected some rocks, but most layers are still horizontal.

The steplike layers of Washington's flood basalt ↘

Some basalt cracked as it cooled. This formed spectacular six-sided columns. ↗

Volcanoes Building Mountains

Volcanic action formed many spectacular mountains of Earth. Most of the peaks formed by volcanoes during the Cenozoic are still visible today.

As we have seen, volcanoes tend to form parallel to a subduction zone. The front edge of a subducted oceanic plate may reach more than 90 miles (150 km) into the mantle. At that point, the heat causes the water content in the rock to separate out and rise. The hot water melts the lithosphere above it. This molten rock also rises into the crust, where it may form a magma chamber. From there, it can ooze or erupt violently.

Volcanoes that form by subduction may be on land or in the ocean. Volcanoes formed from subduction on land are called continental-arc volcanoes. Those that form in the sea are island-arc volcanoes. They are always called "arc" volcanoes because subduction zones are generally curved. They have to follow the spherical shape of Earth.

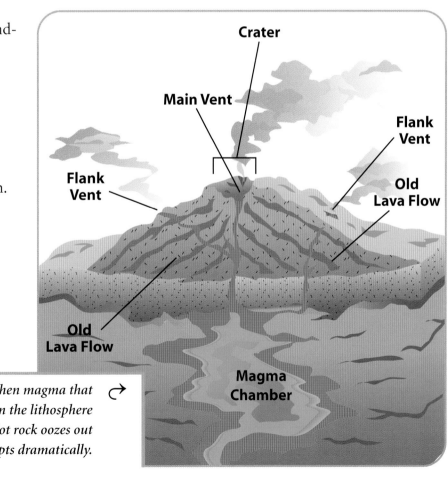

Crater

Main Vent

Flank Vent

Flank Vent

Old Lava Flow

Flank Vent

Old Lava Flow

Magma Chamber

A volcano may form when magma that once filled a chamber in the lithosphere goes to the surface. Hot rock oozes out slowly or erupts dramatically.

THREE FORMS OF VOLCANOES

Shield volcano—a low-lying broad dome formed by slowly flowing lava. These, seen above the clouds, are in Hawaii.

Composite volcano, also called a stratovolcano—cone-shaped, consisting of alternating layers of lava and ash. This one is Mount Shasta in California.

Cinder cone—a cone-shaped pile of ash; usually erodes away fairly quickly. This one is located in Arizona.

Mexico's Mountains

The Cordillera extends south into Mexico. This is where the Sierra Madre ("Mother Mountains") is the main mountain system. (Wyoming also has a small section of the Rockies called the Sierra Madre.) Mexico's Sierra Madre were formed from volcanoes instead of being raised by collision forces. The mountains range up to 12,000 feet (3,666 m) high. Rough canyons make the mountains harsh and inhospitable. The volcanic action in Mexico has not stopped.

The Mexican mountain system is divided into three parts. The westernmost part is called Sierra Madre Occidental. It starts near the United States border and stretches southeast. The volcanoes that formed it erupted mostly during the Cenozoic, between 70 and 20 million years ago.

The easternmost section is called the Sierra Madre Oriental. This is really a continuation of the Cordillera farther north. It parallels the east coast of Mexico. There is a wide coastal plain to the east of these volcanic mountains. Mexico's highest mountain is a volcano called Orizaba. It is 18,855 feet (5,747 m) high. It is located near the east coast, east of Mexico City.

A third section is called Sierra Madre del Sur ("southern"). This is a rugged area south of where the two other sections link up. Between these three ranges lies the Mexican Plateau. It occupies about 40 percent of the country.

Paricutín is a volcano that was "born" in 1943 ↷
in a Mexican farm field. It grew into a mountain
that continued to ooze lava for nine years.

The Sierra Madre Occidental

There are three ranges of mountains in Mexico. The westernmost, the Sierra Madre Occidental (shown in the photo from space), is the most rugged. Most of the rocks that make up the range are of volcanic origin. They were formed primarily in the Cenozoic Era. The land of the Sierra Madre Occidental varies widely. It ranges from high mountain peaks covered with snow year around to hot, tropical valleys.

The Sierra Madre Occidental seen from space ↱

The Copper Canyon region in the north consists of more than 200 canyons. Some of them are deeper than the Grand Canyon. However, those canyons do not show the vast range of geologic history that the Grand Canyon does. They were formed by intense volcanic activity. This activity occurred between 30 and 40 million years ago. Rushing water then eroded the canyons.

The mountain range greatly affects the climate of nearby regions. It acts as a barrier to moisture. The slopes that face the waters of the Gulf of California are covered with vegetation. Meanwhile, slopes facing Mexico's interior, as well as the land to the east, are barren.

In 2000, Popocatepetl, a volcano located just 37 miles (60 km) from Mexico City, erupted. North America's second highest volcano, its name means "smoking mountain." There was no lava when it erupted. Instead, hot gases melted the ice cap on top of the mountain. Deadly mudslides formed. These put thousands of people in danger. However, people continue to live in the danger zone on the mountain.

The Ring of Fire

Mexico's volcanic activity is part of the subduction that is going on around much of the Pacific plate. The active volcanoes make up what has been called the Ring of Fire. This great chain of volcanoes includes Japan, the Philippines, New Zealand, the Andes Mountains of South America, and the Cascade Range of North America.

In South and Central America, the Ring of Fire volcanoes are on land. In the northern Pacific, most of the volcanic action in North America occurs in the Aleutian Island chain. This chain stretches southwestward from mainland Alaska. The chain of visible mountains is about 1,200 miles (1,900 km) long. Other submerged mountains make the chain longer.

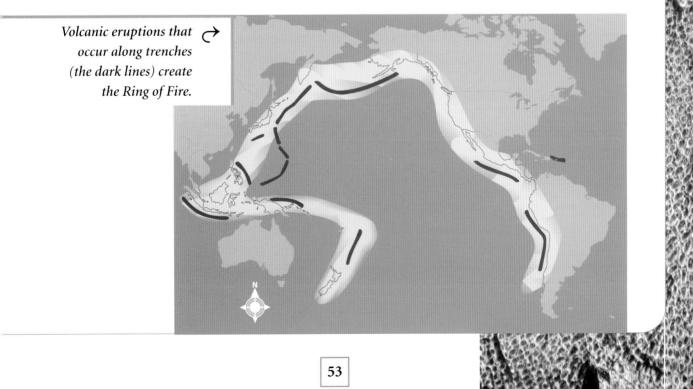

Volcanic eruptions that occur along trenches (the dark lines) create the Ring of Fire.

In the Valley of Ten Thousand Smokes

↳ Mount Katmai in Alaska

Katmai National Park in Alaska is located on the Pacific Ring of Fire. The Alaska Peninsula and its extension, the Aleutian Islands, form the Aleutian Mountain Range of Alaska. The range consists of a series of active volcanoes. These form an island arc that follows the curve of the Aleutian Trench.

The volcanoes of the Aleutians are of the type that often erupt very explosively. Mount Katmai erupted for three days in 1912. It was one of the most violent eruptions of modern time. The top blew off Katmai, creating a **caldera**. A caldera is a huge bowl in the rock. It is many times larger than the actual volcanic vent that created it. A climb to the rim of Mount Katmai shows a caldera over 3 miles (4.8 km) across. The caldera contains two glaciers. These obviously formed after the eruption.

The Valley of the Ten Thousand Smokes is located within Katmai National Park. The "10,000 smokes" are **fumaroles**. Fumaroles are openings in the ground through which volcanic gases and steam escape. The valley shows the deep ash that extends outward from the volcano. Nearby glaciers are also covered by ash. At least 14 volcanoes may still be active within the valley.

HOW DO THEY KNOW
Whether a Volcano is Still Active?

Geologists rely on three tools to tell them if a volcano is active and if it might erupt.

Instruments called seismometers are stationed all around the world to identify earthquakes within the earth. These sensitive instruments can record any deep rumbling within a volcano. Such seismic activity might indicate that magma was on the move. If a volcano has been quiet for a long time, the ink markings on a seismometer (right) may be the first indication that it is becoming active again.

If a volcano starts rumbling, geologists may use another tool, GPS, or the Ground Positioning System, to detect any changes or **deformation** of the ground. This is the same system that uses several satellites (left) to locate cars on highways or hikers in the woods. GPS can detect tiny changes in, for example, the height of a lava dome building up inside the crater of a volcano. If the dome is rising, magma is on the move and is increasing pressure on the ground above it.

Satellite One

Satellite Two

Satellite Three

A third tool is remote sensing for the release of gases from the ground. Small remote-controlled aircraft can be flown over a volcano. They carry little laboratories that measure and record the gases that might be released by magma. An increase in gas release might mean that an eruption is coming. The kinds of gases can tell geologists just what kind of eruption it might be.

These tools are very useful. However, they still cannot give geologists enough information to predict just when an eruption might occur.

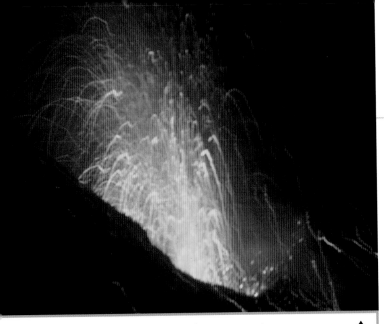

Hawaii's active volcanoes continue to erupt. ↰
The lava collects, forming new land for the state.

The Hawaiian Volcanoes

North America can be thought of as having additional, regularly erupting spectacular volcanoes. This is because Hawaii is part of the United States. However, Hawaii is on the Pacific plate, not the North American.

A heat plume, called a **hot spot**, formed Hawaii's volcanoes. A heat plume forms under a plate, often far from the edges.

The youngest of the Hawaiian Islands is also the largest. This is the island actually called Hawaii, or the Big Island. Nowhere is its rock more than half a million years old. This island is located over a hot spot in the mantle. Two of the volcanoes that built the island of Hawaii are still active. They are Mauna Loa and Kilauea. A new one, called Loihi, has not yet reached above sea level.

The oldest of the Islands is Kure. It lies about 1,500 miles (2,400 km) to the northwest of the island of Hawaii. Even farther northwest are more volcanoes created by the hot spot. These are undersea volcanic mountains called the Emperor Seamounts.

The Hawaiians have different names for different lava. For example, where the molten lava flows smoothly, and then solidifies, a smooth and ropy lava rock is formed. It is called pahoehoe (pronounced "pah-hoe-ee-hoe-ee"). If a thicker lava partially solidifies but then continues to flow, a rough, blocky lava rock forms. Called aa ("ah-ah"), it is very difficult to walk on.

Different Hawaiian lavas—pahoehoe (top) and aa (bottom) ↰

The Largest Mountain

Mauna Kea, an inactive volcano on the island of Hawaii, is considered by many geologists to be the largest mountain on Earth. Its weight depresses the seafloor. As a result, when measured from its base below the seafloor to its top, it comes out an amazing 56,000 feet (17,000 m) high. That's about twice the height of Mount Everest. However, the Himalayas rise from land instead of the sea. Though located near the equator, Mauna Kea has had glaciers on its highest peaks.

North America's Hot Spots

Hot spots can also occur beneath continental crust. North America has been drifting across one for millions of years. It is now located beneath Yellowstone National Park in Montana. The heat from the hot spot creates the **geysers**, mudpots, and hot springs that so fascinate visitors. The last actual volcanic eruption in Yellowstone occurred about 600,000 years ago.

Eighteen million years ago, the Yellowstone hot spot was located beneath where Boise, Idaho, is today. The North American plate was moving across the hot spot. This process formed the 400-mile (644-km)-long Snake River Plain. The plain is a large, flat depression. It makes up about one-fourth of the state of Idaho.

Moving tectonic plates have changed our planet time and again. This has been happening over the 4.6 billion years that Earth has existed. Moving plates and volcanoes continued to build North America's west coast during the Cenozoic. As we'll see in the next chapter, the climate of the continent was also changing, in ways that would affect how we live today.

↻ *Fumaroles are bursts of steam from underground. They show the presence of a hot spot under Yellowstone National Park.*

Chapter 5

Evolving Mammals and the Growing Cold

When the dinosaurs disappeared, mammals came out of hiding. As a result, the Cenozoic became the Age of Mammals. As the Paleocene Epoch started, most mammals were tiny. They were no more than the size of a rat. Many mammals remained small. Examples include rodents and rabbits. Big changes occurred by the end of the Paleocene, however. Some of the largest plant-eaters, or herbivores, that have ever lived had also evolved. Amazingly, both small bats and huge whales all developed within a few million years of the beginning of the Cenozoic.

The Eocene—Mammals Take Over

Many dinosaurs were plant-eaters, or herbivores. When dinosaurs disappeared, various mammals changed their habits. These species had previously been insect-eaters, but they became herbivores.

Among the earliest large plant-eating mammals during the Paleocene Epoch was a group called condylarths. Elephants, aardvarks, rhinoceroses, and horses all stemmed from the condylarths. Rhinos? Yes, much of their development occurred in North America. At least, it was here that most of their fossils have been found.

Among the earlier condylarth fossils found was *Phenacodus*. This Eocene forest-living animal was about the size of a sheep. It had slender legs like a dog and a long tail.

↳ *Artist's drawing of an ancestral rhino*

In the seas, mammals were just getting started. Whales began to develop. No one really knows why mammals went into the sea. Millions of years before, animals moved from the sea to land. This new **evolutionary** change was the exact opposite of that earlier movement.

↵ *A museum painting shows a huge* Uintatherium *pursuing early hoofed mammals, perhaps the ancestors of horses.*

This Eocene whale, Basilosaurus, was descended from mammals that returned to the sea after living on land for millions of years. A fossil tooth of a whale is below.

The oldest known whales belong to a family called Archaeocetes. Such whales may have developed from a wolflike animal. They still had legs. It is not known whether they continued to climb out onto land. Many of the first fossils have been found in deposits that would have been made in freshwater, instead of seawater.

Vertebrates—animals with backbones—were also taking over the air during the Eocene. Within that epoch, most modern bird families appeared. The largest flying bird ever known was *Argentavis*, found in Argentina. It had a wingspan of more than 25 feet (7.6 m). Its flight feathers may each have been up to 5 feet (1.5 m) long.

Most very large birds did not fly. Instead, they lived their lives restricted to the ground. *Diatryma* was a meat-eating bird. It stood up to 9 feet (2.7 m) high. It lived in the Wyoming area at the beginning of the Eocene Epoch. *Gastronis* was a large flightless bird that lived during later years. It was present in both eastern and western North America. It was a little shorter than *Diatryma*. Despite its size, it was powerful and fast enough to hunt down horses.

Interestingly, bats, too, got their start during the Eocene. Fossils of these early flying mammals have been found in the southwestern United States.

Mesembriornis was a huge flesh-eating bird of the Pliocene. It was probably an ancestor of today's rhea, a flightless bird.

Grasslands: A Changed World

At the start of the Cenozoic Era, Earth was still a greenhouse world. Warm, moist forests and jungles were everywhere. They were the primary habitat of many mammals. The primary land plants were the flowering plants, or angiosperms.

During the Eocene Epoch, the planet began to cool. Seafloor spreading had slowed down. As a result, the sea became cooler. That, in turn, made the land climate cooler. The change to a cooler climate helped the grasses, another kind of angiosperm, evolve. They became plants that were capable of covering vast areas of land. Where there had previously been forests there were now grasslands, in both temperate and subtropical regions. Today, every continent has grasslands.

The development of grasslands would seem to be helpful to large plant-eating mammals. Instead, many such mammals became extinct. The grasses making up these new grasslands were tougher than previous grasses. They were also tougher than the leaves that the browsing animals generally ate.

Some tough plants of the North American grasslands

The new grasses contained more of the mineral called silica. This mineral had a tendency to grind down an animal's teeth. Some animals had no way to replace worn teeth. As a result, these animals soon died out. They were replaced by other groups of animals with stronger teeth. One group was the ancestral elephants.

The first known ancestral elephant lived during the Eocene Epoch in Africa. It did not look at all like modern elephants. It was only 3 feet (1 m) high. It weighed no more than 265 pounds (120 kg). Its descendants spread throughout Europe, Asia, and North America. Mammoths and mastodons were elephants known by the early North American Indians.

Much more widespread, though, was another group of mammals that was descended from the condylarths. These were the **ungulates**, which means "hoofed."

This ungulate, or hoofed mammal, from the Miocene had a tiny hoof on each of its toes. Hoofs gave animals an advantage in running on grassland.

Hoofed Animals on the Grasslands

The ungulates gradually divided into two groups. The division was based on the number of toes they had. Horses, rhinos, and tapirs had an odd-number of toes. Later, the even-toed ungulates—cattle, sheep, camel—got their start.

It seems odd today to think of rhinoceroses in North America. Even so, a number of rhinoceroslike hoofed animals roamed the forests of the Eocene. One of them, the *Uintatherium*, had three pairs of horns. These were like knobs, projecting from its head (see page 58). This mammal measured 13 feet (4 m) long. Like carnivores, it had long, sharp canine teeth. It was a herbivore, however.

The big titanotheres were similar to rhinoceroses. Fossils have been found throughout northern North America. They were found especially in the Badlands of South Dakota, California, and up into central Canada. These animals evolved to great size rapidly during the Eocene. They disappeared almost as rapidly.

↳ *A bed of rhinoceros fossil bones from the Miocene*

Teleoceros was a North American rhinoceros. It appears to have lived much of its time in water. This is just as hippopotamuses do today. Fossil skeletons of these rhinos have been unearthed from Florida to California. ↱

↳ Prairie of the
North American central plains

Animals of the Grasslands

Fossil evidence shows that all modern families of plants had evolved by the Miocene Epoch. This includes flowering plants. An important group of flowering plants of that time were the grasses. Plains and prairies of grass spread over much of North America.

A great variety of grazing mammals evolved during that time. Many of them developed longer limbs and foot bones. These traits helped provide the greater speed that they would need to escape predators on the open grasslands. For greater speed, some ran on their toes. Some even developed hoofs to protect the toe bones. Their teeth adapted to the task of almost constant grazing of touch grasses.

The seeds of the grasses were also useful as food. Seeds sustained many new and different rodents, insects, and birds. There were also animals that preyed on the grazers and seed-eaters. These predators had to develop stealth and speed to catch their prey.

Fossil teeth from the Miocene show that horses had developed teeth for grinding grasses. ↳

Bison are wild cattle that lived on the North American prairie. ↳

The first horselike animals lived in western North America about 55 million years ago. They were sometimes called eohippus, meaning, "dawn horse." Today, they are officially called *Hyracotherium*.

Horses were not much larger than small dogs. They gradually grew larger and lost toes. The foot evolved to become a single toe encased in a protective hoof.

At first, horses were forest-dwellers. However, they eventually moved out onto the grasslands. During the Miocene, horses developed teeth that continued to grow as the tough grasses they ate wore them down. Finally, less than 5 million years ago, the modern horse *(Equus)* appeared.

As horses evolved, they crossed the Bering land bridge, which was land that once connected North America and Asia. After crossing into Asia, horses spread to all continents except Australia and Antarctica. Eventually, the lives of horses in North America ended. This was the result of humans, disease, and climate change. Horses disappeared from the North American scene about 8,000 years ago. They did not reappear until the Spanish brought domesticated horses from Europe in A.D. 1500.

↺ Orohippus, *four-toed horse of the Paleocene*

↺ Pliohippus *of the Pliocene was the first one-toed horse (left). It was the "grandfather" of today's modern horse , called* Equus *(right).*

Horses, rhinos, and tapirs are the only odd-toed ungulates. More successful in sheer numbers were even-toed ungulates. One group of even-toed ungulates developed digestive systems with multiple stomachs. Cattle, camels, goats, and sheep have the ability to live on nothing but grasses. This is possible due to bacteria within their stomachs. The bacteria break down the cell walls of the tough leaves.

Camels evolved in North America. Sometime during the Eocene, they split into two groups. Both of these groups eventually migrated to other continents. This left North America with no camels.

One group became smaller camellike animals. These are present now in South America. They include llamas, alpacas, vicuñas, and guanacos. The other group crossed the Bering land bridge into Asia. From there they spread into Africa and the Middle East, where camels are still found today.

North American camels of the Miocene, before they migrated to other lands

The Predators

Animals that grazed on open grasslands became runners. This is because predators had also developed. Predators, by their nature, are meat-eaters, or carnivores. They need to be fast. Those mammals described as belonging to the carnivore family include cats, dogs, bears, and weasels.

An ancestral cat, Dinictis, of the Oligocene, preying on early horses

Predators need strong, sharp teeth for tearing the flesh of their prey. One Eocene cat, *Eusmilus*, had long, curved saberlike teeth. It wasn't a true sabertoothed cat, however. They came later.

Unlike cats, the dog ancestors developed great endurance. They tired their prey to death. Both cats and dogs evolved into many varieties. Most did not survive to recent times to become those species that humans domesticated as pets and helpers. There are many more species of wild cats alive today than there are dog species.

The carnivore family also includes seals. These probably evolved from a mammal similar to an otter. Both seals and otters spend part of their lives on land and part in water. Their high-speed legs have evolved into flippers. Their family name, Pinnipedia, means "fin-foot." They all have thick layers of fat on their bodies. This fat protects them in the cold of the ocean.

↺ *Seals are carnivores that can occupy icy places because of the fat on their bodies.*

Primates

Primates are monkeys, apes, and humans. The first primates began to evolve after the K-T Extinction. Early primates may have resembled the aye-aye. This animal still lives in Madagascar. It is quite small with very large eyes.

Like horses and rhinos, primates got a strong start in North America. Then they disappeared, probably by the middle of the Oligocene Epoch. However, they remained in South America.

For many years, scientists assumed that New World (South American) monkeys and Old World (African and South Asian) monkeys had evolved in parallel fashion. They thought the same thing was happening separately on each continent. More recently, though, they have been able to check the genes in the animals. Now they think that the two continents' monkeys came from the same ancestors.

Suppose the two groups of monkey do have a common ancestor. It follows that there must have been some physical land links between South America and Africa. Some geologists think that perhaps there may have been islands above sea level along the seafloor-spreading ridge in the South Atlantic. Ancestral monkeys could then have island-hopped between Africa and South America.

A fossil primate was found in northern Ethiopia in 1974. It is officially called *Australopithecus afarensis,* meaning "southern ape from Afar." It is better known as Lucy, after the Beatles song "Lucy in the Sky with Diamonds." The primate lived 3.2 million years ago. The partial skeleton showed many humanlike, or hominid, characteristics. Therefore it would be put into a new line of primate evolution. This line is separate from the monkeys and chimpanzees. These hominid characteristics included a knee structure that meant Lucy walked upright.

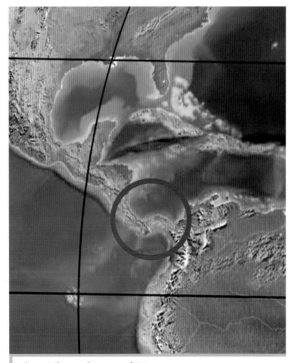

↥ *The Isthmus of Panama connects North and South America.*

Connecting North and South

North America and South America had been connected during the Jurassic Period but then separated. Starting about 20 million years ago, they began to approach each other again. By 3.5 million years ago, the tapered bottom of North America touched the top of South America. This created the Isthmus of Panama. It provided a highway for living things between continents. This movement has been called the Great American Interchange.

There was more movement from north to south. As a result, many southern species were made extinct by the invasion of northern animals into the south. Primates and camels moved into South America. There they evolved into the species known today.

Into the North

The traffic wasn't all one way. Some animals from South America moved into North America. Among them were giant furry creatures called ground sloths. Today's South American mammals called sloths are fairly small, gentle, slow-moving animals. They live in trees, where they hang upside down. They are very different from ancestral sloths.

In the late Miocene, four species of large ground sloths moved into southern North America. Fossils of sloths 20 feet (6 m) long have been found. These animals could stand on their hind legs. When standing, they were as tall as the giraffes we know now. They weighed more than 3 tons (2.7 tonnes). They had massive claws, which they used in defense, not eating. *Megatherium*, the giant ground sloth, had huge claws that kept it from putting its front feet on the ground. Ground sloths were able to survive the Ice Age. They became extinct about 12,000 years ago.

↥ *A ground sloth stood to eat leaves off trees. It had claws so big that it could not run.*

Other mammals came into North America at about the same time as the big sloths. These included capybaras, anteaters, armadillos, and even vampire bats. All these except armadillos moved completely to the south again when the Ice Age started.

↰ *The nine-banded armadillo is an insect-eater that moved north from South America.*

A Cooling Planet

The temperature of the planet was gradually cooling during the Cenozoic Era. In the Miocene Epoch, Antarctica became completely isolated from both Australia and South America. That separation allowed a new ocean current to form. It formed a wall around the south polar continent that prevented warmer tropical water from mixing with the cold water around Antarctica. An important result was the buildup of an ice cap.

The new Isthmus of Panama also created a barrier. Ocean currents in the Atlantic could no longer go beyond this barrier. An entirely new circulation pattern developed in the oceans of the world. The Gulf Stream that warms western Europe developed as a result of the new circulation pattern. But this new pattern also allowed the Arctic Ocean to freeze. Glaciers formed on the land that bordered the Arctic.

The gradual drop in temperature probably didn't occur smoothly. Scientists think that it dropped in a series of steps. Between those steps, there were periods of warmth. Even Antarctica had forests growing in it.

HOW DO THEY KNOW
Earth's Temperature was Gradually Cooling?

Samples of the ocean floor are called **cores**. They have been drilled in all the major oceans of the world. These core samples have been tested by biologists, geologists studying layers of rock, climate experts, and other specialists. Mostly they look for changes in **species** that formed fossils in the rocks. They also look for quantity of the microscopic floating organisms called **plankton**.

Scientists examine core samples for important plankton organisms. These include one-celled animals called **foraminiferans** and one-celled plants called **coccoliths**. Both creatures produce external or internal shells. These shells accumulate on the ocean floor. As temperatures go down even the slightest bit, the proportions of the different species found in the seafloor rock also change.

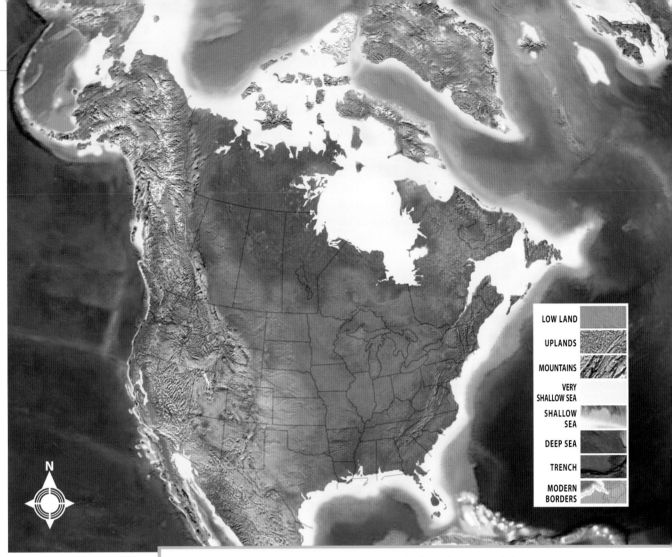

↳ *North America, 2 million years ago, before the start of the Ice Age*

Each time a glacial period began, Antarctica began to cool before the Arctic. By about 4 million years ago, the Arctic Ocean and Greenland were covered with ice, as they are today.

The Cenozoic Era is not yet over. The era started out with Earth as a tropical place. Fossils of tropical plants have been found as far north as Canada. Alligators lived in the Arctic. But throughout the 63 million years of the Tertiary, Earth was gradually cooling.

The period of heaviest glaciation called the Ice Age did not begin until most recent times. This is the case even though the ice actually began to form during the Pliocene. A time of ice, a time in which we still live, was about to begin.

GEOLOGIC TIME SCALE

PRECAMBRIAN TIME • 4.5 billion to 543 million years ago

Time Period	Tectonic Events	Biological Events
Hadean Eon *4.5–3.96 billion years ago* Named for Hades, or Hell	No Earth rocks from this time found	None
Archean Eon *3.96–2.5 billion years ago* Name means "Ancient"	Oldest known rocks First permanent crust First stable continents	Seawater formed First bacteria Atmosphere formed
Proterozoic Eon *2.5 billion–543 million*	North American craton formed First iron–bearing sediments First large glaciation Formation and breakup of Rodinia supercontinent Gondwana, southern supercontinent, formed	Free oxygen in atmosphere First nucleated cells, allowing sexual reproduction First multicellular animals First animals with exoskeletons First fungi

PHANEROZOIC TIME • 543 million years ago to present

PALEOZOIC ERA • 543 to 248 million years ago

Time Period	Tectonic Events	Biological Events
Cambrian Period *543–248 million years ago* Named for old name of Wales	Laurentia separated from Siberia	Cambrian Explosion: Major diversification of marine invertebrates
Ordovician Period *490–443 million years ago* Named for a Celtic tribe in Wales	First Iapetus Ocean Taconic orogeny in northeastern Laurentia	First true vertebrates: jawless fish First land plants Mass extinction
Silurian Period *443–417 million years ago* Named for a Celtic tribe in Wales	Caledonian orogeny Shallow seas on Laurentia	First vascular plants First insects First jawed fish
Devonian Period *417–354 million years ago* Named for Devon, England	Major reef building	First forests First seed–baring plants First four–footed animals First amphibians
CARBONIFEROUS PERIOD *354 to 290 million years ago* — **Mississippian Epoch** *354–323 million years ago* Named for Mississippi River Valley	Antler orogeny	Ferns abundant First land vertebrates
Pennsylvanian Epoch *323–290 million years ago* Named for coal formations in Pennsylvania	Appalachian orogeny began Antler orogeny	Ferns abundant Major coal–forming forests First reptiles
Permian *290–248 million years ago* Named for Russian province of Perm	Pangea formed	First warm–blooded reptiles Greatest mass extinction

	Time Period	Tectonic Events	Biological Events
MESOZOIC ERA 248 to 65 million years ago	**Triassic Period** *248–206 million years ago* Named for three layers in certain European rocks	Pangea completed Major part of Pangea was arid	First flying vertebrates First dinosaurs First mammals Cephalopods abundant
	Jurassic Period *206–144 million hears ago* Named for the Jura Mountains	Atlantic began to open Pangea separated into Gondwana and Laurasia	First birds Cycads abundant
	Cretaceous Period *144–65 million years ago* Named after Latin word for "chalk"	Major volcanism Sevier orogeny Laurentia separated from Eurasia Sierra Nevada batholith	First flowering plants First social insects Mass extinction of dinosaurs

	Time Period	Tectonic Events	Biological Events
TERTIARY PERIOD 65 to 1.8 million years ago	**Paleocene Epoch** *65 to 54.8 million years ago*	Laramide orogeny Western Laurentia uplifted	Mammals and birds diversified First horse ancestors
	Eocene Epoch *54.8 to 33.7 million years ago*	Rockies uplifted Global cooling began	First mammals (whales) in sea First primates First cats and dogs
	Oligocene Epoch *33.7 to 23.8 million years ago*	North Atlantic opened Ice cap formed in Anatarctica	First apes Grasslands widespread
	Miocene Epoch *23.8 to 5.3 million years ago*	Columbia flood basalts	First human ancestors First mastodons
	Pliocene Epoch *5.3 to 1.8 million years ago*	Northern Hemisphere glaciation began Cascade Volcanoes	Large mammals abundant
QUATERNARY PERIOD 1.8 million to today	**Pleistocene Epoch** *1.8 million years ago to today*	Great glaciation of Northern Hemisphere	First modern humans Extinction of large mammals Humans entered North America
	Holocene *10,000 years ago to today*	Rifting continued in East Africa Human–caused global warming	Human-caused extinctions

PHANEROZOIC TIME • 543 million years ago to present

CENOZOIC ERA • 65 million years ago to present

accretion the addition of terrane to a larger tectonic plate; typically occurs as a result of subduction

adaptability the qualities of a living thing that allow it to accept major changes in its environment or habitat

angiosperm a flowering plant. Angiosperms develop a seed within a case, called an ovary, which turns into fruit. Many important crops are angiosperms.

asthenosphere the part of Earth's mantle that lies beneath the lithosphere. This zone of soft, easily deformed rock is believed to be less rigid, hotter, and more fluid than the rock above or below.

badlands heavily eroded barren land

basalt dark, dense volcanic, igneous rock. Basalt makes up most of the ocean floor.

basin a low area, or depression, in the earth's surface, usually where sediment collects.

batholith a large body of igneous rock that crystallizes deep beneath the earth's surface as hardened magma

bedrock the bottom or lowest layer of rock; solid rock that lies beneath soil and other loose surface materials

bolide any object in the solar system other than planets, such as comets, meteorites, and asteroids, especially one that strikes Earth

calcite mineral made of calcium carbonate ($CaCO_3$); the principal component of limestone and chalk

caldera a usually circular crater formed by the collapse of the top of a volcano after the magma chamber has emptied out

coal sedimentary rock derived from partially decomposed, carbonized plant matter. This black or dark brown mineral substance is used as fuel.

Coastal Plain a generally flat area of sedimentary rock along a seacoast between hard rock and the ocean. Capitalized, the plain along the east and southern coast of the United States; without capitals, any such plain.

coccolith limestone scale or plate formed by single-celled algae that are part of plankton. Sometimes both the algae and their scales are called coccoliths.

comet a large ball made of ice and dust that circles the sun in the solar system in a predicable orbit

conifer a type of tree, such as pines, that is generally evergreen, has needle-like leaves, and bears seeds on cones

Cordillera the region of North America made up of the entire chain of mountain ranges parallel to the Pacific Coast, from Mexico to Alaska

core 1) the interior part of Earth beginning at about 1,800 miles (2,900 km) below Earth's surface. Composed mostly of iron and nickel, it is divided into two parts: the outer core, which is mostly liquid, and the inner core, which is solid. 2) a cylindrical sample of rock or ice obtained by a special drill

crater a usually circular depression, either in the top of a volcano or formed by the impact of a meteorite

craton the usually stable, unchanging mass of rock that forms the basic central mass of a continent

Cretaceous-Tertiary Extinction event that occurred 65 million years ago during which the dinosaurs became extinct or died off quickly. In addition to the dinosaurs, about 55% of all species were wiped out. Also called the K-T Extinction.

crust outermost, rocky layer of Earth. This low-density layer is about 22 miles (35 km) thick under continents and 6 miles (10 km) thick under oceans.

deformation the changes in shape, dimension, or volume of rocks that result from folding, faulting, and other processes

divergent moving away from each other. Divergent boundaries between tectonic plates are called passive margins and sediment usually accumulates

epoch a division of geologic time next shorter than a period, especially in the Cenozoic Era

era a division of geologic time next smaller than the eon and larger than a period. For example, the Cenozoic Era is in the Phanerozoic Eon and includes the Miocene Epoch.

evolution the development of a species or other group of organisms; the theory that all existing organisms are related and that they developed from earlier forms

exotic terrane small landmass, or terrane, that has been transported into its present setting from some distance and is very different in character from the land to which it is attached

extinction the complete disappearance of a species of plant or animal from the earth

fault a fracture, or break, in rock along which each side moves relative to each other. Sudden movements along a fault creates earthquakes.

fault-block mountains mountains created by large-scale normal faulting

flood basalt rock produced by massive oozing from large cracks in the earth's crust

floodplain the usually flat area alongside a river or stream which floods when water levels are high

fold a noticeable curve in the layering of sedimentary or metamorphic rock; large-scale folding can create mountains.

fold thrust a fold in sedimentary rock that has been pushed horizontally over other land

foraminiferan (or **foram**) a marine protozoan that typically has a linear, spiral, or concentric shell. Pseudopodia (literally meaning "false feet") extend through small holes or pores in the shell.

fossil evidence or trace of animal or plant life of a past geological age. These typically mineralized remains have been preserved in rocks of the earth's crust. These traces include bones and footprints of extinct land animals, such as dinosaurs.

fumarole a vent in the ground through which steam or gases escape, usually near a volcano

geologic time scale a calendar that establishes distinct time periods in the history of the earth. The time is shown in millions of years. The geologic time scale used in this book is on pages 72 and 73.

geyser a hot spring that sends up jets of hot water and steam into the air intermittently

glaciation the process of becoming covered by ice or glaciers. It refers to a period of geological time when global cooling occurred and ice sheets covered large areas of the earth.

glacier a mass of dense ice on land that moves slowly, either by coming down from high mountains or by spreading out across land from a central point where the ice has accumulated

Gondwana supercontinent in the Southern Hemisphere that began to separate from Pangea toward the end of the Paleozoic Era. It contained present-day South America, Africa, southern Europe, India, Australia, and Antarctica.

granite coarse-grained, intrusive, igneous rock. Granite is composed of sodium and potassium feldspar primarily, but it is also rich in quartz. Light in color, it is a common rock.

heat plume column of hot material in the earth's mantle that rises toward the lithosphere; also called a mantle plume

hot spot a site of volcanism that is not located near the boundary of a tectonic plate. The Hawaiian Islands were created by a hot spot under the Pacific plate.

Ice Age span of geological time during the Pleistocene Epoch when much of the Northern Hemisphere was covered with ice sheets

igneous rock rock formed directly from magma when it has cooled and solidified (crystallized). *Igneous* means "fiery."

intrusive formed by the movement of magma into another, already existing rock. Batholiths are intrusive.

island arc a curved or arc-shaped chain of volcanic islands lying near a continent, formed as a result of subduction, such as the Aleutian Islands in Alaska

Laurentia a continent formed during Precambrian times from which the modern continent of North America developed. It was composed mostly of North America and Greenland, parts of northwestern Scotland, and Scandinavia.

lava fluid, molten rock, or magma, that emerges from a volcano or volcanic vent to the earth's surface. When cooled and solidified, it is igneous rock such as basalt.

limestone a type of sedimentary rock, made up of more than 50% calcium carbonate ($CaCO_3$), primarily as calcite. It may be mixed with sediments or mud.

lithosphere the hard outer layer of Earth containing the outer part of Earth's mantle and its crust. It consists of tectonic plates that move across the surface of Earth.

magma molten rock that exists beneath the earth's crust. Magma that reaches the surface is called lava.

mammal a warm-blooded vertebrate animal that feeds its young on its mother's milk; includes both pouched and nonpouched animals

mantle the thick part of Earth's interior that lies between the crust and the outer core. Along with the crust, the upper mantle forms tectonic plates.

marine relating or pertaining to the sea

marsupial a mammal that bears its young immature. The young complete their development inside a pouch on the mother's abdomen. Marsupials include the opossum and kangaroo.

mass extinction event during the earth's history when many species of living things became extinct, or were killed off, due to drastic changes in the environment

metamorphic rock any rock that has been created by a chemical or structural change to rock that already exists. This change may be due to variations in temperature, pressure and other geological conditions.

meteorite mass of matter that has reached Earth from outer space

molten liquefied by heat

mudstone a hardened, claylike sedimentary rock with the texture of shale

normal fault a fault in which the rock on one side slides down the slope of the rock on the other side; it's no more normal than any other kind of fault.

orogeny process by which mountains are built. This process involves folding, faulting, and uplifting of the earth's crust.

Pangea (also written **Pangaea**) the supercontinent made up of most landmasses and covering about 25 percent of Earth's surface. Formed by the end of the Paleozoic Era, it lasted more than 100 million years.

period a division of an era. A period may include several smaller geologic time units called epochs.

Permian Extinction time at the end of the Paleozoic Era when almost all living things became extinct, or died out. Scientists estimate that almost 95% of all animal and plant species were wiped out. It is also known as the Permian-Triassic (P-T) Extinction.

placental mammal warm-blooded vertebrate with a four-chambered heart. It is characterized by a covering of hair on some or most of its body. It nourishes its young with milk from mammary glands.

plankton organisms, such as microscopic algae and protozoa, that passively float or drift within a body of water and feed many animals

plateau a large area of uplifted rock that appears to be fairly flat on top

province a generally large area of crust in which the rock has undergone about the same geologic history

reef large mound or ridge within a body of water, made from the skeletons of organisms such as corals and sponges cemented together

reptile an air-breathing vertebrate (animal with a backbone) that lives on land, including snakes, turtles, lizards, crocodiles, as well as other extinct creatures.

rift a long, narrow crack in the entire thickness of the earth's crust. To rift means to split the earth's crust. Rifting that continues a long time will create new tectonic plates.

seafloor spreading the process that occurs as new crust is formed at a spreading ridge under the ocean and two tectonic plates are pushed apart by great quantities of new volcanic rock. Continents riding on these plates are also pushed apart.

sediment loose, uncemented pieces of rock or minerals carried and deposited by water, air, or ice. Sediment may include eroded sand, dirt particles, debris from living things, and solid materials that form as a result of chemical processes.

sedimentary rock rock composed of hardened sediment. Examples include sandstone and limestone. Sedimentary rock typically forms beds, or layers.

shale finely layered sedimentary rock derived from mud; formed by the consolidation of clay, mud, or silt. About 70% of all of Earth's sedimentary rock is shale.

silica silicon dioxide (SiO_2) compounds that often take a crystalline form. Silica especially occurs as quartz, sand, flint, and agate. Almost 60% of Earth's crust is silica, and it is found in about 95% of Earth's rocks.

species the smallest category of plant or animal. One or more species are included in a genus. Members of a species tend to interbreed only with each other.

spreading ridge undersea area where seafloor spreading occurs. The ridges form an irregular line on the ocean floor of the entire planet. Lava rises at these ridges and pushes plates apart to form new seafloor.

strike-slip fault a fault in which one section of rock slides past another without any change in elevation

subduction the process by which oceanic crust moves down into the asthenosphere beneath a continental plate; occurs at trenches, called subduction zones

supercontinent a giant temporary landmass made up of several present-day continents, such as Gondwana and Pangea

tectonic plate large section of Earth's lithosphere that floats on the asthenosphere and moves independently, with plates sometimes rubbing against each other

terrane a fragment of crust that is bounded on all sides by faults and which has a geologic history that differs from neighboring blocks. It may be made from island arcs or a piece of a tectonic plate.

thrust fault a type of fault in which the plane of the fracture is fairly small. On a large scale, it can send a great deal of rock horizontally over other rock.

topography detailed mapping or charting of the features of a relatively small area

transform fault a vertical fracture in which rock on one side slides past the other. Transform faults connect ocean ridges because of the curve of Earth's surface.

trap a dark colored, fine-grained igneous rock, such as basalt. Traps have a steplike appearance. The term comes from the Swedish word *trapp* for "staircase."

tundra the region toward the poles where only low-growing plants can survive in the soil that thaws in the summer but remains frozen underneath

ungulate a mammal with hoofs on its feet; includes sheep, horses, pigs, camels, and others

uplift process in which a portion of the earth's crust is raised as a result of heat within the mantle. The crust can also be raised in response to tectonic forces, or large-scale movements deep within Earth.

FURTHER INFORMATION

ONLINE WEB SITES

Museum of Paleontology
University of California at Berkeley
1101 Valley Life Sciences Building
Berkeley, CA 94720
www.ucmp.berkeley.edu/exhibit/exhibits.html
takes you through major exhibits in geology,
evolution, and the classification of living things
Also produced by UCMP is:
www.paleoportal.org
provides a link to many sites for anyone
interested in paleontology

United States Geological Survey
USGS National Center
12201 Sunrise Valley Drive
Reston, VA 20192
www.usgs.gov/education
The Learning Web introduces numerous topics and
projects related to earth science
Find out what's happening at Mount St. Helens
volcano: http://volcanoes.usgs.gov
or where the earthquakes are:
http://earthquake.usgs.gov

The British Broadcasting Corporation has major coverage of prehistoric life:
http://www.bbc.co.uk

MUSEUMS

Be sure to look for museum web sites. Also, be sure to check university and public
museums in your area; they often have good geology exhibits.

UNITED STATES
American Museum of Natural History
Central Park West at 79th St.
New York, NY 10024
www.amnh.org

Colorado School of Mines Geology Museum
13th and Maple St.
Golden, CO 80401

The Field Museum
1400 S. Lake Shore Drive
Chicago, IL 60605
www.fieldmuseum.org
Look for the online exhibit about Sue, the best
preserved *Tyrannosaurus rex*

University of Michigan Museum of Paleontology
1109 Geddes Ave.,
Ann Arbor, MI 48109
www.paleontology.lsa.umich.edu

Smithsonian National Museum of Natural History
10th St. and Constitution Ave.
Washington, D.C. 20560
www.mnh.si.edu

CANADA
Geological Survey of Canada
Earth Sciences Sector
601 Booth St.
Ottawa, Ontario K1A 0E8, Canada
http://ess.nrcan.gc.ca

Canadian Museum of Nature
240 McLeod St.
Ottawa, Ontario K1P 6P4, Canada
www.nature.ca

Provincial Museum of Alberta
12845 102nd Ave.
Edmonton, Alberta T5N 0M6, Canada
www.prma.edmonton.ab.ca

Manitoba Museum of Man and Nature
190 Rupert Avenue
Winnipeg, Manitoba R3B 0N2, Canada
www.manitobamuseum.mb.ca

Pacific Museum of the Earth
6339 Stores Road
Vancouver, British Columbia V6T 1Z4, Canada
www.eos.ubc.ca

DVDs

Amazing Earth, Artisan Entertainment, 2001

Forces of Nature—Book and DVD, National Geographic, 2004

Living Rock: An Introduction to Earth's Geology, WEA Corp, 2002
Also includes 400 USGS "Fact Sheets" in Adobe Acrobat format, obtainable on computer sytems with a DVD-ROM Drive)

Physical Geography: Geologic Time, TMW/Media Group, 2004

Volcano: Nature's Inferno!, National Geographic, 1997

BOOKS

Anderson, Peter. *A Grand Canyon Journey: Tracing Time in Stone.* A First Book. Danbury, CT: Franklin Watts, 1997.

Ball, Jacqueline. *Earth's History.* Discovery Channel School Science series. Milwaukee, WI: Gareth Stevens Publishing, 2004.

Bonner, Hannah. *When Bugs Were Big : Prehistoric Life in a World Before Dinosaurs.* Washington, DC: National Geographic, 2004.

Castelfranchi, Yuri, and Nico Petrilli. *History of the Earth: Geology, Ecology, and Biology.* Hauppage, NY: Barrons, 2003.

Colson, Mary. *Earth Erupts.* Turbulent Earth series. Chicago: Raintree, 2005.

Colson, Mary. *Shaky Ground.* Turbulent Earth series. Chicago: Raintree, 2005.

Day, Trevor. *DK Guide to Savage Earth: An Earth Shattering Journey of Discovery.* New York: Dorling Kindersley, 2001.

Farndon, John. *How the Earth Works.* Pleasantville, NY: Reader's Digest, 1992.

Hooper, Meredith. *The Pebble in My Pocket: A History of Our Earth.* New York: Viking Books, 1996.

Lambert, David. *The Kingfisher Young People's Book of the Universe.* Boston: Kingfisher, 2001.

Maslin, Mark. *Earthquakes.* Restless Planet series. Chicago: Raintree, 2000.

Maynard, Christopher. *My Book of the Prehistoric World.* Boston: Kingfisher, 2001.

Oxlade, Chris. *The Earth and Beyond.* Chicago: Heinemann Library, 1999.

INDEX